The Beatles
A-I

T0088601

ISBN 978-1-4234-9466-9

HAL•LEONARD®
CORPORATION
7777 W. BLUEMOUND RD. P.O. BOX 13819 MILWAUKEE, WI 53213

For all works contained herein:
Unauthorized copying, arranging, adapting, recording, Internet posting, public performance,
or other distribution of the printed music in this publication is an infringement of copyright.
Infringers are liable under the law.

Visit Hal Leonard Online at
www.halleonard.com

Contents

How to Use This Book

Piano Chord Songbooks include the lyrics and chords for each song.
The melody of the first phrase of each song is also shown.

First, play the melody excerpt to get you started in the correct key.
Then, sing the song, playing the chords that are shown above the lyrics.

Chords can be voiced in many different ways. For any chords that are
unfamiliar, refer to the diagram that is provided for each chord. It shows
the notes that you should play with your right hand. With your left hand,
simply play the note that matches the name of the chord. For example,
to play a C chord, play C-E-G in your right hand, and play a C in your
left hand.

You will notice that some chords are *slash chords*; for example, C/G.
With your right hand, play the chord that matches the note on the left side
of the slash. With your left hand, play the note on the right side of the
slash. So, to play a C/G chord, play a C chord (C-E-G) in your right hand,
and play a G in your left hand.

All Together Now

Words and Music by John Lennon
and Paul McCartney

Melody:

One, two, three, four,

F♯   G   D7   C6   D6

C♯   F♯   A♯   D   G   B   C D   F♯   A   C   E   G A   D   F♯   A B

Intro   F♯‖: G | | | :‖

Verse 1
> **G**   **D7**
> One, two, three, four, can I have a little more?
>
> **G**   **D7**   **G**
> Five, six, seven, eight, nine, ten, I love you.

Verse 2
> **G**   **D7**
> A, B, C, D, can I bring my friend to tea?
>
> **G**   **D7**   **G**
> E, F, G, H, I, J, I love you.

Bridge 1
> **G**
> (Boom, boom, boom,
>
> **C6**
> Boom, boom, boom.) Sail the ship,
>
> **G**
> (Boom, boom, boom.) Chop the tree,
>
> **C6**
> (Boom, boom, boom.) Skip the rope,
>
> **D6**   **D7**
> (Boom, boom, boom.) Look at me!
>
> (All together now.)

Copyright © 1968, 1969 Sony/ATV Music Publishing LLC
Copyright Renewed
All Rights Administered by Sony/ATV Music Publishing LLC, 8 Music Square West, Nashville, TN 37203
International Copyright Secured   All Rights Reserved

Chorus 1

G
All together now, (All together now.)

All together now, (All together now.)

D7
All together now, (All together now.)

G
All together now. (All together now.)

Verse 3

G   **D7**
Black, white, green, red, can I take my friend to bed?

G   **D7**   **G**
Pink, brown, yellow, orange and blue, I love you.

(All together now.)

Chorus 2

    G
‖: All together now, (All together now.)

All together now, (All together now.)

D7
All together now, (All together now.)

G
All together now. (All together now.) :‖

Bridge 2   *Repeat Bridge 1*

Chorus 3
         G
‖: All together now, (All together now.)

All together now, (All together now.)
D7
All together now, (All together now.)
G
All together now. (All together now.) :‖

Chorus 4
         G
All together now, (All together now.)

All together now, (All together now.)
D7
All together now, (All together now.)
         G
All together now.

Across the Universe

Words and Music by John Lennon
and Paul McCartney

Words are flow-ing out __ like end - less...

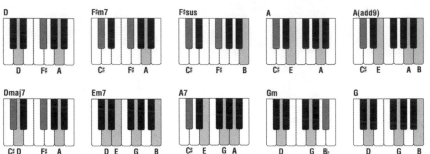

Intro

| D | F#m F#sus F#m F#sus F#m F#sus F#m F#sus |

| A A(add9) A A(add9) A A(add9) A A(add9) |

Verse 1

D   Dmaj7 F#m
Words are flowing out__ like endless rain into a paper cup,

 Em7   A7
They slither while they pass they slip away__ across the universe.

D   Dmaj7   F#m
Pools of sorrow, waves of joy are drifting through my open mind,

 Em7   Gm
Pos-sessing and ca-ressing me.

Chorus 1

D   A7
Jai. Guru. Deva. Om.

Nothing's gonna change my world,

G   D
Nothing's gonna change my world.

A7
Nothing's gonna change my world,

G   D
Nothing's gonna change my world.

Copyright © 1968, 1970 Sony/ATV Music Publishing LLC
Copyright Renewed
All Rights Administered by Sony/ATV Music Publishing LLC, 8 Music Square West, Nashville, TN 37203
International Copyright Secured   All Rights Reserved

Verse 2

D   Dmaj7   F#m   Em7
Images of broken light which dance before me like a million eyes,

                         A7
They call me on and on across__ the universe.

D   Dmaj7   F#m
Thoughts meander like a restless wind inside a letter box,

   Em7   A7
They tumble blindly as they make their way across the universe.

Chorus 2   *Repeat Chorus 1*

Verse 3

D   Dmaj7   F#m
Sounds of laughter, shades of life are ringing through my open ears,

   Em7   Gm
In-citing and in-viting me.

D   Dmaj7   F#m   Em7
Limitless, un-dying love which shines around me like a million suns,

            A7
It calls me on and on a-cross the universe.

Chorus 3   *Repeat Chorus 1*

Outro

   D
‖: Jai. Guru. Deva.:‖   *Play 6 times and fade*

All I've Got to Do

Words and Music by John Lennon
and Paul McCartney

Melody:

When-ev-er I...

Intro | E |

Verse 1
     C#m   **E**
Whenever I _____ want you a-round, yeah,
     C#m **F#m**
All I gotta do _____ is call you on the phone

And you'll come running home,
     Am   **E**
Yeah, that's all I _____ gotta do.

Verse 2
     C#m   **E**
And when I, _____ I wanna kiss you, yeah,
     C#m **F#m**
All I gotta do _____ is whisper in your ear

The words you long to hear,
     Am **E**
And I'll _____ be kissing you.

Copyright © 1963, 1964 Sony/ATV Music Publishing LLC
Copyright Renewed
All Rights Administered by Sony/ATV Music Publishing LLC, 8 Music Square West, Nashville, TN 37203
International Copyright Secured   All Rights Reserved

Chorus 1

                                    A
And the same goes for me,

Whenever you want me at all,

   C#m
I'll be here, yes I will, whenever you call,

    A   E C#m
You just gotta call on me, yeah,

    A   E
You just gotta call on me.

Verse 3

N.C.   C#m   E
And when I, _____ I wanna kiss you, yeah,

    C#m   F#m
All I gotta do _____ is call you on the phone

And you'll come running home,

   Am   E
Yeah, that's all I _____ gotta do.

Chorus 2

                                      A
And the same goes for me,

Whenever you want me at all,

   C#m
I'll be here, yes I will, whenever you call,

    A   E C#m
You just gotta call on me, yeah,

    A   E
You just gotta call on me.

    A   E
You just gotta call on me.

Outro

    C#m E C#m
Mm.   *Fade out*

All My Loving

Words and Music by John Lennon
and Paul McCartney

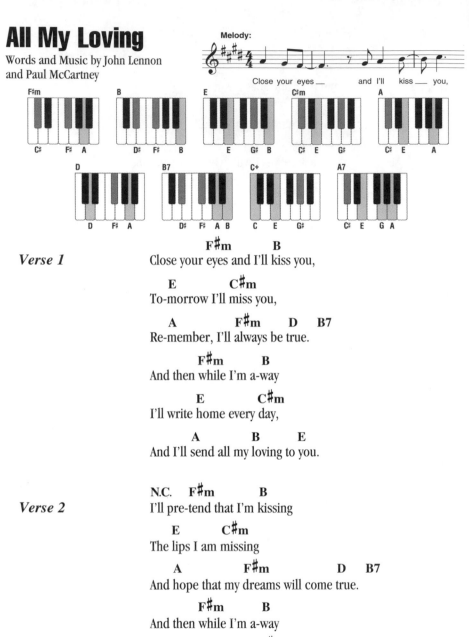

Melody:

Close your eyes ___ and I'll kiss ___ you,

Verse 1

        F♯m   **B**
Close your eyes and I'll kiss you,

    E   **C♯m**
To-morrow I'll miss you,

   A   **F♯m**   **D** **B7**
Re-member, I'll always be true.

   F♯m   **B**
And then while I'm a-way

     E   **C♯m**
I'll write home every day,

     A   **B**   **E**
And I'll send all my loving to you.

Verse 2

  N.C. **F♯m**   **B**
I'll pre-tend that I'm kissing

    E   **C♯m**
The lips I am missing

   A   **F♯m**   **D** **B7**
And hope that my dreams will come true.

   F♯m   **B**
And then while I'm a-way

     E   **C♯m**
I'll write home every day,

     A   **B**   **E**
And I'll send all my loving to you.

Copyright © 1963, 1964 Sony/ATV Music Publishing LLC
Copyright Renewed
All Rights Administered by Sony/ATV Music Publishing LLC, 8 Music Square West, Nashville, TN 37203
International Copyright Secured   All Rights Reserved

Chorus 1

      C#m C+   E
All my loving I will send to you,

      C#m C+   E
All my loving, darling, I'll be true.

Solo

| A7 | | E | | |
| B7 | | E | | |

Verse 3

N.C.   F#m   B
Close your eyes and I'll kiss you,

     E   C#m
To-morrow I'll miss you,

     A   F#m   D   B7
Re-member, I'll always be true.

       F#m   B
And then while I'm a-way

       E   C#m
I'll write home every day,

       A   B   E
And I'll send all my loving to you.

Chorus 2

      C#m C+   E
All my loving I will send to you,

      C#m C+   E
All my loving, darling, I'll be true.

      C#m
All my loving,

     E
All my loving, oo-ooh,

      C#m
All my loving

       E
I will send to you.

All You Need Is Love

Words and Music by John Lennon
and Paul McCartney

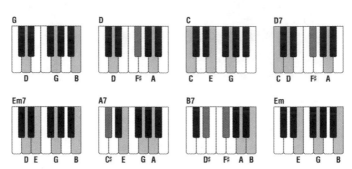

Intro
|G   D |G |C   D7 |

G   D   Em7
Love, love, love,

G   D   Em7
Love, love, love,

D7/A G   D7/F♯ D7/E
Love, love, love.

|D   D/C |D |

Verse 1

G   D/F♯   Em7
  There's nothing you can do that can't be done,

G   D/F♯   Em7
  Nothing you can sing that can't be sung,

D7/A   G
  Nothing you can say,

              D/F♯   D7/E
But you can learn how to play the game,

    D   D/C   D
It's easy.

Copyright © 1967 Sony/ATV Music Publishing LLC
Copyright Renewed
All Rights Administered by Sony/ATV Music Publishing LLC, 8 Music Square West, Nashville, TN 37203
International Copyright Secured   All Rights Reserved

Verse 2

    G   D/F♯   Em7
    Nothing you can make that can't be made,

    G   D/F♯   Em7
    No one you can save that can't be saved,

D7/A   G
Nothing you can do,

          D/F♯   D7/E
But you can learn how to be you in time,

      D   D/C   D
It's easy.

Chorus 1

    G   A7   D   D7
    All you need is love,

    G   A7   D   D7
    All you need is love,

    G   B7   Em Em7
    All you need is love, love,

C   D7   G
Love is all you need.

  G   D Em7
(Love, love, love.)

  G   D Em7
(Love, love, love.)

  D7/A G   D7/F♯   D7/E
(Love, love, love.)

|D   D/C|D |

	G A7 D D7

Chorus 2

> G   A7   D   D7
> All you need is love,
>
> G   A7   D   D7
> All you need is love,
>
> G   B7   Em Em7
> All you need is love, love,
>
> C   D7   G
> Love is all you need.

Verse 3

> G   D/F$\sharp$ Em7
> There's nothing you can know that isn't known,
>
> G   D/F$\sharp$ Em7
> There's nothing you can see that isn't shown,
>
> D7/A   G
> There's nowhere you can be
>
>   D/F$\sharp$ D7/E
> That isn't where you're meant to be,
>
>   D   D/C   D
> It's easy.

Chorus 3   *Repeat Chorus 2*

Chorus 4   *Repeat Chorus 2*

Outro

> G
> Love is all you need.
>
> (Love is all you need.)
>
> ‖: Love is all you need.
>
> (Love is all you need.) :‖   ***Repeat and fade***

The Ballad of John and Yoko

Words and Music by John Lennon
and Paul McCartney

Stand-ing   in   the   dock   at   South Hamp - ton,

E	E7	A	B7	E6
E G♯ B	D E G♯ B	C♯ E A	D♯ F♯ A B	C♯ E G♯ B

Intro |E | |

Verse 1

    E
Standing in the dock at South Hampton,

Trying to get to Holland or France.
    E7
The man in the mac said,

"You've got to go back,"

You know they didn't give us a chance.

Chorus 1

    A
Christ! You know it ain't easy,

    E
You know how hard it can be,

    B7
The way things are going,

    E
They're gonna crucify me.

Copyright © 1969 Sony/ATV Music Publishing LLC
Copyright Renewed
All Rights Administered by Sony/ATV Music Publishing LLC, 8 Music Square West, Nashville, TN 37203
International Copyright Secured   All Rights Reserved

Verse 2	**E** Finally made the plane into Paris,
	Honeymooning down by the Seine.
	E7 Peter Brown called to say,
	"You can make it OK,
	You can get married in Gibraltar, near Spain."
Chorus 2	*Repeat Chorus 1*
Verse 3	**E** Drove from Paris to the Amsterdam Hilton,
	Talking in our beds for a week.
	E7 The newspeople said,
	"Say, what you doing in bed?"
	I said, "We're only trying to get us some peace."
Chorus 3	*Repeat Chorus 1*
Bridge	**A** Saving up your money for a rainy day,
	Giving all your clothes to charity.
	Last night the wife said,
	"Oh boy, when you're dead,
	B7 You don't take nothing with you but your soul."
	Think!

Verse 4

E
Made a lightning trip to Vienna,

Eating chocolate cake in a bag.

E7
The newspapers said,

"She's gone to his head,

They look just like two gurus in drag."

Chorus 4

Repeat Chorus 1

Verse 5

E
Caught the early plane back to London,

Fifty acorns tied in a sack.

E7
The men from the press said,

"We wish you success,

It's good to have the both of you back."

Chorus 5

A
Christ! You know it ain't easy,

E
You know how hard it can be,

B7
The way things are going,

E
They're gonna crucify me.

B7
The way things are going,

E
They're gonna crucify me.

| B7 | | | E | | E6 |

And I Love Her

Words and Music by John Lennon
and Paul McCartney

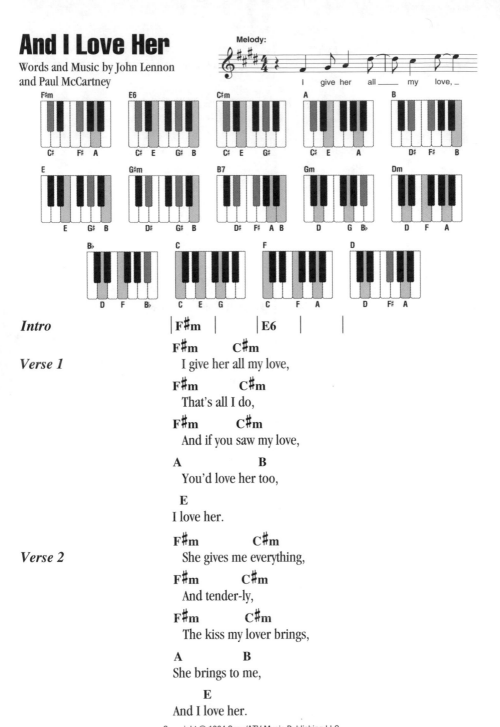

Intro |F#m | |E6 | | |

Verse 1

   F#m   C#m
I give her all my love,

   F#m   C#m
That's all I do,

   F#m   C#m
And if you saw my love,

   A   B
You'd love her too,

    E
I love her.

Verse 2

   F#m   C#m
She gives me everything,

   F#m   C#m
And tender-ly,

   F#m   C#m
The kiss my lover brings,

   A   B
She brings to me,

    E
And I love her.

Copyright © 1964 Sony/ATV Music Publishing LLC
Copyright Renewed
All Rights Administered by Sony/ATV Music Publishing LLC, 8 Music Square West, Nashville, TN 37203
International Copyright Secured   All Rights Reserved

Bridge

C#m   B
A love like ours

C#m   G#m
Could never die

C#m   G#m
As long as I

         B   B7
Have you near me.

Verse 3

F#m   C#m
Bright are the stars that shine,

F#m   C#m
Dark is the sky,

F#m   C#m
I know this love of mine

A   B
Will never die,

     E
And I love her.

Interlude

| Gm | Dm | Gm | Dm | Gm |
| Dm | Bb | C | F | |

Verse 4

Gm   Dm
Bright are the stars that shine,

Gm   Dm
Dark is the sky,

Gm   Dm
I know this love of mine

Bb   C
Will never die,

     F
And I love her.

Outro

| Gm | | F | | |
| Gm | | D | |

And Your Bird Can Sing

Words and Music by John Lennon
and Paul McCartney

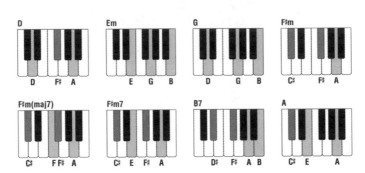

Intro
|D | | | |

Verse 1

D
Tell me that you've got everything you want,

And your bird can sing,

            Em
But you don't get me,

G   D
  You don't get me.

Verse 2

D
You say you've seen seven wonders,

And your bird is green,

            Em
But you can't see me,

G   D
  You can't see me.

Copyright © 1966 Sony/ATV Music Publishing LLC
Copyright Renewed
All Rights Administered by Sony/ATV Music Publishing LLC, 8 Music Square West, Nashville, TN 37203
International Copyright Secured   All Rights Reserved

Bridge 1

F#m   F#m(maj7)
When your prized pos-sessions

F#m7   B7
Start to weigh you down,

D   Em
Look in my di-rection,

                 A
I'll be 'round, I'll be 'round.

Solo

| D | | | |
| Em | G | D | |

Bridge 2

F#m   F#m(maj7)
When your bird is broken,

F#m7   B7
Will it bring you down?

D   Em
You may be a-woken,

                 A
I'll be 'round, I'll be 'round.

Verse 3

         D
You tell me that you've heard every sound there is,

And your bird can swing,

           Em
But you can't hear me,

G   D
   You can't hear   me.

Outro

D			
Em	G	D	
			G/D

Another Girl

Words and Music by John Lennon
and Paul McCartney

Melody:

For I have got... ___

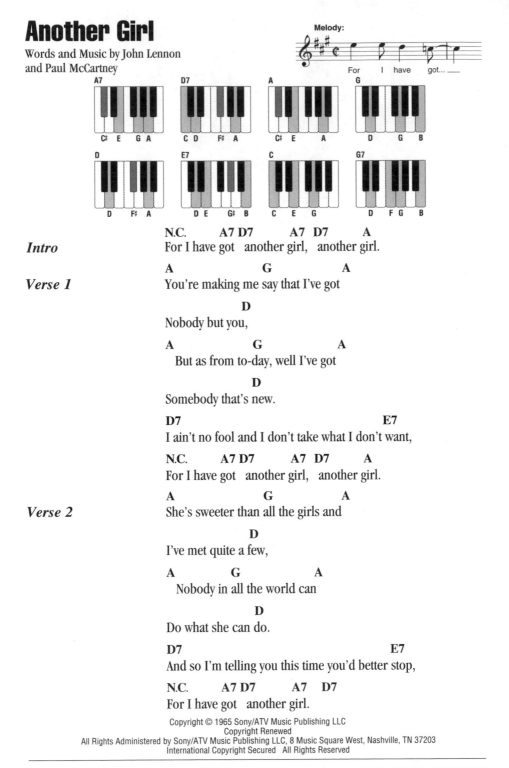

Intro

N.C.   A7 D7   A7 D7   A
For I have got another girl, another girl.

Verse 1

A   G   A
You're making me say that I've got

            D
Nobody but you,

A   G   A
  But as from to-day, well I've got

            D
Somebody that's new.

D7   E7
I ain't no fool and I don't take what I don't want,

N.C.   A7 D7   A7 D7   A
For I have got another girl, another girl.

Verse 2

A   G   A
She's sweeter than all the girls and

            D
I've met quite a few,

A   G   A
  Nobody in all the world can

            D
Do what she can do.

D7   E7
And so I'm telling you this time you'd better stop,

N.C.   A7 D7   A7 D7
For I have got another girl.

Copyright © 1965 Sony/ATV Music Publishing LLC
Copyright Renewed
All Rights Administered by Sony/ATV Music Publishing LLC, 8 Music Square West, Nashville, TN 37203
International Copyright Secured All Rights Reserved

Bridge 1

       C   G7   C
Another girl who will love me till the end,

G7   C
   Through thick and thin,

      E7   A   E7
  She will always be my friend.

Verse 3

A   G   A
  I don't wanna say that I've been

           D
Unhappy with you,

A   G   A
  But as from to-day, well, I've seen

           D
Somebody that's new.

D7   E7
I ain't no fool and I don't take what I don't want,

N.C.   A7 D7   A7   D7
For I have got   another girl.

Bridge 2   *Repeat Bridge 1*

Verse 4

A   G   A
  I don't wanna say that I've been

           D
Unhappy with you,

A   G   A
  But as from to-day, well I've seen

           D
Somebody that's new.

D7   E7
I ain't no fool and I don't take what I don't want,

N.C.   A7 D7   A7
For I have got   another girl.

D7   A7 D7   A
  Another girl,   another girl.

Anytime at All

Words and Music by John Lennon
and Paul McCartney

Melody:

An - y - time   at   all, _____

Chorus 1

       Bm D
Anytime at all,

       A
Anytime at all,

       Bm
Anytime at all,

             G
All you've got to do is call

      A   **Dsus D Dsus2 D**
And I'll be there.

Verse 1

D   **F#m/C#**
If you need some-body to love,

Bm   **Gm/B♭**
Just look into my eyes,

D/A   **A**   **D**
I'll be there to make you feel right.

Verse 2

D   **F#m/C#**
If you're feeling sorry and sad,

Bm   **Gm/B♭**
I'd really sympa-thize.

D/A   **A**   **Dsus D Dsus2 D**
Don't you be sad, just call me to-night.

Copyright © 1964 Sony/ATV Music Publishing LLC
Copyright Renewed
All Rights Administered by Sony/ATV Music Publishing LLC, 8 Music Square West, Nashville, TN 37203
International Copyright Secured   All Rights Reserved

Chorus 2   *Repeat Chorus 1*

Verse 3
    D   F#m/C#
    If the sun has faded away,

    Bm   Gm/B♭
    I'll try to make it shine.

    D/A   A   D
    There is nothing I won't do.

Verse 4
    D   F#m/C#
    When you need a shoulder to cry on,

    Bm   Gm/B♭
    I hope it will be mine.

    D/A   A   Dsus D Dsus2 D
    Call me tonight, and I'll come to you.

Chorus 3   *Repeat Chorus 1*

Solo
| A | A7 | A | A7 | G | A | |
| G | A | Dsus D Dsus2 | D | | | |

Chorus 4
    N.C.   Bm D
    Anytime at all,

         A
    Anytime at all,

         Bm
    Anytime at all,

              G
    All you've got to do is call

     A   Dsus D Dsus2 D
    And I'll be there.

         G
    Anytime at all,

            A
    All you've got to do is call

     A   Dsus D Dsus2 D
    And I'll be there.

Ask Me Why

Words and Music by John Lennon
and Paul McCartney

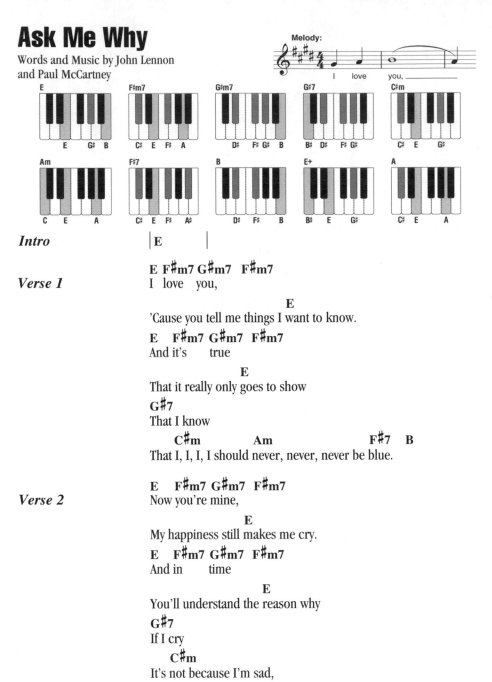

Intro | E |

Verse 1

E F#m7 G#m7 F#m7
I love   you,

                                    E
'Cause you tell me things I want to know.

E   F#m7 G#m7 F#m7
And it's   true

                          E
That it really only goes to show

G#7
That I know

        C#m   Am   F#7   B
That I, I, I, I should never, never, never be blue.

Verse 2

E   F#m7 G#m7 F#m7
Now you're mine,

                          E
My happiness still makes me cry.

E   F#m7 G#m7 F#m7
And in   time

                          E
You'll understand the reason why

G#7
If I cry

     C#m
It's not because I'm sad,

                    Am   E   E+
But you're the only love that I've ever had.

Copyright © 1962 UNIVERSAL/DICK JAMES MUSIC LTD., JULIAN LENNON, SEAN ONO LENNON and YOKO ONO LENNON
Copyright Renewed
All Rights for the U.S. and Canada Controlled and Administered by UNIVERSAL - SONGS OF POLYGRAM INTERNATIONAL, INC.
All Rights Reserved   Used by Permission

Bridge 1

<pre>
                      A   B   E   E+
          I can't be-lieve   it's happened to me,
                          A   B   E N.C.
          I can't con-ceive   of any more   misery.
</pre>

Chorus 1

<pre>
          E   F#m7 G#m7
          Ask me   why,
                   A
          I'll say I love you
                   G#m7   A   E
          And I'm always thinking of you.
</pre>

Verse 3   *Repeat Verse 1*

Chorus 2

<pre>
          E   F#m7 G#m7
          Ask me   why,
                   A
          I'll say I love you
                   G#m7   A   E   E+
          And I'm always thinking of you.
</pre>

Bridge 2   *Repeat Bridge 1*

Chorus 3

<pre>
          E   F#m7 G#m7
          Ask me   why,
                   A
          I'll say I love you
                   G#m7   A   E
          And I'm always thinking of you.
          A   E
          You,
          A   G#m7
          You.
</pre>

Baby You're a Rich Man

Words and Music by John Lennon
and Paul McCartney

Melody:

How does it feel _____ to be...

| G | C | G7 | F | B♭6 |

Intro

|G |C/G |G |C/G |G7 |C/G |G7 |C/G |

Verse 1

G   C/G   G7
How does it feel to be one of the beautiful people?

G   F/G
Now that you know who you are,

F   G   C
What do you want to be?

G   F/G
And have you traveled very far?

F   G   C
Far as the eye can see.

Verse 2

G   C/G   G7
How does it feel to be one of the beautiful people?

G   F/G
How often have you been there?

F   G   C
Often enough to know.

G   F/G
What did you see when you were there?

F   G   C
Nothing that doesn't show.

Copyright © 1967 Sony/ATV Music Publishing LLC
Copyright Renewed
All Rights Administered by Sony/ATV Music Publishing LLC, 8 Music Square West, Nashville, TN 37203
International Copyright Secured   All Rights Reserved

Chorus 1

G
Baby, you're a rich man,

C
Baby, you're a rich man,

G   C
Baby, you're a rich man, too.

Bb6   G7/B   C
You keep all your money in a big brown bag

      G7
Inside a zoo.

               C
What a thing to do.

G
Baby, you're a rich man,

C
Baby, you're a rich man,

G   C
Baby, you're a rich man, too.

Verse 3

G   C/G   G7
How does it feel to be one of the beautiful people?

G   F/G
Turned to a natural E,

F   G   C
Happy to be that way.

G   F/G
Now that you've found another key,

F   G   C
What are you going to play?

Chorus 2   *Repeat Chorus 1*

Outro

G
‖: Baby, you're a rich man,

C
Baby, you're a rich man,

G   C
Baby, you're a rich man, too. :‖ *Repeat and fade*

Baby's in Black

Words and Music by John Lennon
and Paul McCartney

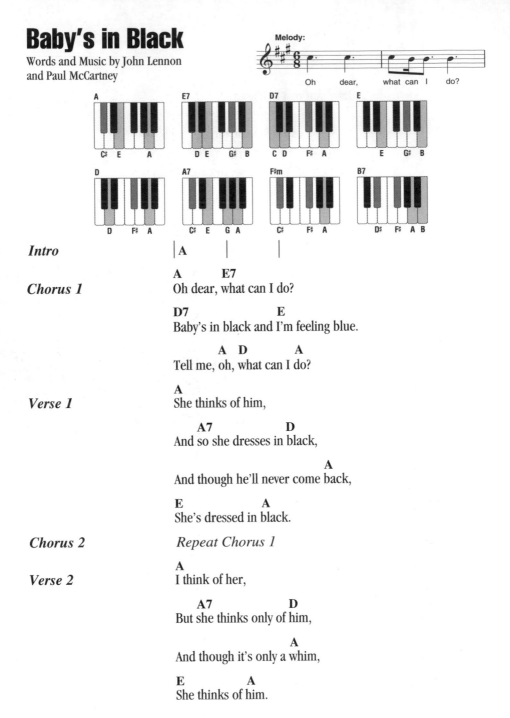

Melody:

Oh dear, what can I do?

Intro

|A | | |

Chorus 1

A   E7
Oh dear, what can I do?

D7   E
Baby's in black and I'm feeling blue.

          A   D   A
Tell me, oh, what can I do?

Verse 1

A
She thinks of him,

        A7   D
And so she dresses in black,

                              A
And though he'll never come back,

E   A
She's dressed in black.

Chorus 2

Repeat Chorus 1

Verse 2

A
I think of her,

        A7   D
But she thinks only of him,

                            A
And though it's only a whim,

E   A
She thinks of him.

Copyright © 1964 Sony/ATV Music Publishing LLC
Copyright Renewed
All Rights Administered by Sony/ATV Music Publishing LLC, 8 Music Square West, Nashville, TN 37203
International Copyright Secured   All Rights Reserved

	F#m B7
Bridge 1	Oh, how long will it take,
	D E7 A
	Till she sees the mistake she has made?

	A E7
Chorus 3	Oh dear, what can I do?
	D7 E
	Baby's in black and I'm feeling blue.
	A D A
	Tell me, oh, what can I do?

Solo	|A |E |D |E |A D |A |

	F#m B7
Bridge 2	Oh, how long will it take,
	D E7 A
	Till she sees the mistake she has made?

	E7
Chorus 4	Dear, what can I do?
	D7 E
	Baby's in black and I'm feeling blue,
	A D A
	Tell me, oh, what can I do?

	A
Verse 3	She thinks of him,
	A7 D
	And so she dresses in black,
	A
	And though he'll never come back,
	E A
	She's dressed in black.

Chorus 5	*Repeat Chorus 1*

Back in the U.S.S.R.

Words and Music by John Lennon
and Paul McCartney

Melody:

Flew in from Mi - am - i Beach, B.   O.   A.   C.,___

Intro | E7 | | | |

Verse 1
A   D
Flew in from Miami Beach, B.O.A.C.,

C   D
Didn't get to bed last night.

A   D
On the way the paper bag was on my knee,

C   D
Man, I had a dreadful flight.

Chorus 1
                                        A
I'm back in the U.S.S.R.,

C   D
   You don't know how lucky you are, boy.

N.C.   A   E7
Back in the U.S.S.R.

Verse 2
A   D
Been away for so long I hardly knew the place,

 C   D
Gee it's good to be back home.

A   D
Leave it till tomorrow to un-pack my case,

C   D
Honey, disconnect the phone.

Copyright © 1968 Sony/ATV Music Publishing LLC
Copyright Renewed
All Rights Administered by Sony/ATV Music Publishing LLC, 8 Music Square West, Nashville, TN 37203
International Copyright Secured   All Rights Reserved

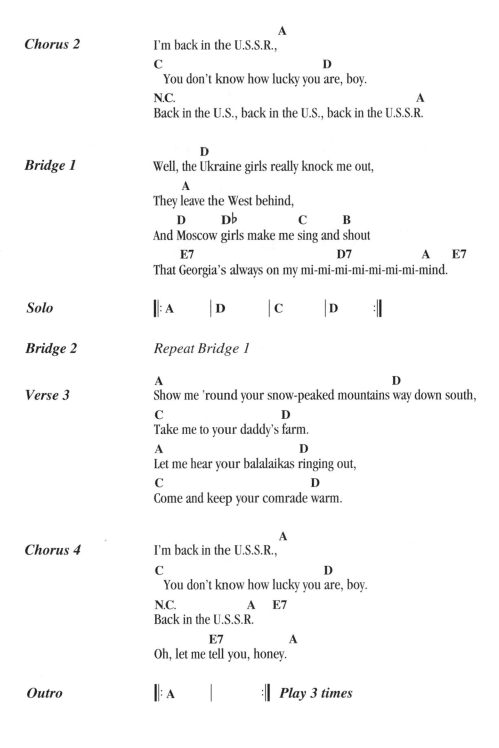

Chorus 2

A
I'm back in the U.S.S.R.,
C   D
  You don't know how lucky you are, boy.
N.C.   A
Back in the U.S., back in the U.S., back in the U.S.S.R.

Bridge 1

D
Well, the Ukraine girls really knock me out,
A
They leave the West behind,
D   D♭   C   B
And Moscow girls make me sing and shout
E7   D7   A   E7
That Georgia's always on my mi-mi-mi-mi-mi-mi-mi-mind.

Solo

‖: A | D | C | D   :‖

Bridge 2

Repeat Bridge 1

Verse 3

A   D
Show me 'round your snow-peaked mountains way down south,
C   D
Take me to your daddy's farm.
A   D
Let me hear your balalaikas ringing out,
C   D
Come and keep your comrade warm.

Chorus 4

A
I'm back in the U.S.S.R.,
C   D
  You don't know how lucky you are, boy.
N.C.   A   E7
Back in the U.S.S.R.
E7   A
Oh, let me tell you, honey.

Outro

‖: A | :‖ *Play 3 times*

Because

Words and Music by John Lennon
and Paul McCartney

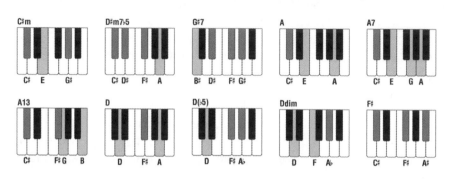

Intro

| C#m | | | D#m7♭5 | G#7 | |

| A | C#m | A7 | A13 | |

D   D(♭5) Ddim
Ah.

Verse 1

      C#m
Be-cause the world is round

       D#m7♭5 G#7
It turns me on,

    A   **C#m**   **A7**   **A13**
Be-cause the world is round,

D D(♭5) Ddim
Ah.

Copyright © 1969 Sony/ATV Music Publishing LLC
Copyright Renewed
All Rights Administered by Sony/ATV Music Publishing LLC, 8 Music Square West, Nashville, TN 37203
International Copyright Secured   All Rights Reserved

Verse 2

       C#m
Be-cause the wind is high

        D#m7b5 G#7
It blows my mind,

    A   C#m A7   A13
Be-cause the wind is high,

D D(b5) Ddim
Ah.

Bridge

Ddim   o   F#
Love is old, love is new,

        G#7
Love is all, love is you.

Verse 3

       C#m
Be-cause the sky is blue

        D#m7b5 G#7
It makes me cry,

    A   C#m A7   A13
Be-cause the sky is blue,

D D(b5) Ddim
Ah.

Outro

C#m		D#m7b5	G#7	
(Ah.)		(Ah.)		
A	C#m	A7	A13	
(Ah.)		Ah.		
D	D(b5)	Ddim		
Ah.				

Being for the Benefit of Mr. Kite

Words and Music by John Lennon
and Paul McCartney

Melody:

For the ben-e-fit ___ of Mis-ter Kite, _

Bb   A   Dm   G   Cm

D F Bb   C# E A   D F A   D G B   C Eb G

G+   Dm7   Gm   Dm(maj7)   Dm6

D# G B   C D F A   D G Bb   C# D F A   D F A Bb

B   Em   Em7   C

D# F# B   E G B   D E G B   C E G

Intro | Bb | A | Dm G |

| Cm   G+
Verse 1   For the benefit of Mr. Kite,

Bb   Dm   G   G+
There will be a show tonight on the trampoline.

          Cm   G+
The Hendersons will all be there,

Bb   Dm   A
Late of Pablo Fanque's fair, what a scene!

          Dm   Dm7
Over men and horses, hoops and garters,

Bb   A   Dm
Lastly through a hogshead of real fire!

          Gm   A   Dm
In this way, Mr. K. will challenge the world.

| Gm A | Dm G |

Copyright © 1967 Sony/ATV Music Publishing LLC
Copyright Renewed
All Rights Administered by Sony/ATV Music Publishing LLC, 8 Music Square West, Nashville, TN 37203
International Copyright Secured   All Rights Reserved

Verse 2

      Cm   **G+**
The celebrated Mr. K.

      B♭   **Dm**   **G**   **G+**
Per-forms his feat on Saturday at Bishopsgate.

      Cm   **G+**
The Hendersons will dance and sing

    B♭   **Dm**   **A**
As Mr. Kite flies through the ring, don't be late!

        Dm   **Dm7**
Messers K. and H. as-sure the public

B♭   **A**   **Dm**
Their production will be second to none.

      Gm   **A**
And of course, Henry the Horse dances the waltz!

Solo 1

```
|Dm  Dm(maj7)|Dm7 Dm6|A       |        |
|Dm  Dm(maj7)|Dm7 Dm6|B       |Em  Em7 |
|C   B  |Em  Em7 |C   B   |Em  |G       |
```

Verse 3

      Cm   **G+**
The band begins at ten to six,

      B♭   **Dm**   **G**   **G+**
When Mr. K. per-forms his tricks with-out a sound.

      Cm   **G+**
And Mr. H. will demonstrate

     B♭   **Dm**   **A**
Ten sommersets he'll undertake on solid ground.

      Dm   **Dm7**
Having been some days in preparation,

  B♭   **A**   **Dm**
A splendid time is guaranteed for all.

      Gm   **A**   **Dm** **Gm** **A**
And to-night Mr. Kite is topping the bill.

Solo 2

```
|Dm  Dm(maj7)|Dm7 Dm6|A       |        |
|Dm  Dm(maj7)|Dm7 Dm6|B       |
||:Em  Em7 |C   B   |Em  Em7 |C   B   :||Em
```

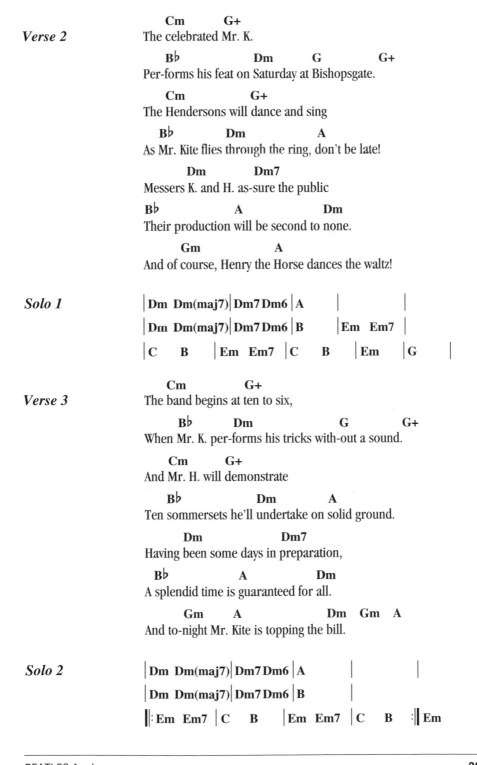

Birthday

Words and Music by John Lennon
and Paul McCartney

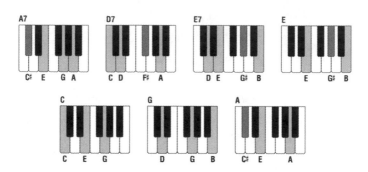

Intro |A7 | | |D7 | |

            |A7 | |E7 | |A7 | |

Verse 1

A7   N.C.
You say it's your birthday,

A7 N.C.
It's my birthday too, yeah.

D7   N.C.
You say it's your birthday,

A7   N.C.
We're gonna have a good time.

E7   N.C.
I'm glad it's your birthday,

A7   N.C.
Happy Birthday to you.

Interlude 1 |***Drums for 8 bars*** |E | | |

Copyright © 1968 Sony/ATV Music Publishing LLC
Copyright Renewed
All Rights Administered by Sony/ATV Music Publishing LLC, 8 Music Square West, Nashville, TN 37203
International Copyright Secured   All Rights Reserved

Bridge 1

     E
Yes, we're going to a party, party,

Yes, we're going to a party, party,

Yes, we're going to a party, party.

C   G
I would like you to dance,

C   G
(Birthday.) Take a cha-cha-cha-chance,

C   G
(Birthday.) I would like you to dance,

C   G   E
(Birthday.) Dance!

Interlude 2

A7			D7	
A7	E7		A7	
A	G	A		G

Bridge 2

C   G
I would like you to dance,

C   G
(Birthday.) Take a cha-cha-cha-chance,

C   G
(Birthday.) I would like you to dance,

C   G   E
(Birthday.) Dance!

Verse 2

A7
You say it's your birthday,

It's my birthday too, yeah.

D7
You say it's your birthday,

A7
We're gonna have a good time.

E7
I'm glad it's your birthday,

A7   A
Happy Birthday to you.

Blackbird

Words and Music by John Lennon
and Paul McCartney

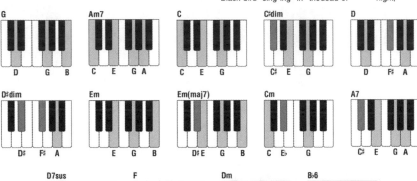

Black-bird sing-ing in the dead of night,

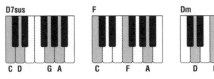

Intro
| G   Am7   G/B | G | |

Verse 1

G   Am7   G/B G
Blackbird singing in the dead of night,

C   C#dim   D   D#dim Em Em(maj7)
Take these broken wings__ and learn__ to fly.

D C#dim C Cm
All your   life,

G/B   A7   D7sus   G
You were only wait - ing for this mo - ment to arise.

| C G/B A7 | D7sus   G | |

Verse 2

G   Am7   G/B G
Blackbird singing in the dead of night,

C   C#dim   D   D#dim Em Em(maj7)
Take these sunken eyes__ and learn__ to see.

D C#dim C Cm
All your   life,

G/B   A7   D7sus   G
You were only wait - ing for this mo - ment to be free.

Copyright © 1968, 1969 Sony/ATV Music Publishing LLC
Copyright Renewed
All Rights Administered by Sony/ATV Music Publishing LLC, 8 Music Square West, Nashville, TN 37203
International Copyright Secured   All Rights Reserved

Bridge 1

F   C/E Dm C   B♭6 C
Black - bird,____ fly.

F   C/E Dm C   B♭6 A7
Black - bird,____ fly.

            D7sus   G
Into the light_____ of a dark black night.

Interlude 1

| G Am7 G/B | G | C C♯dim D D♯dim | Em Em(maj7) |
| D   C♯°dim | C Cm | G/B A7 | D7sus4 G |

Bridge 2

Repeat Bridge 1

Interlude 2

| G Am7 G/B | G | | |
| G Am7 G/B C | G/B A7 D7sus |

Verse 3

G   Am7   G/B   G
Blackbird singing in the dead of night,

C   C♯dim   D   D♯dim Em Em(maj7)
Take these broken wings__ and learn__ to fly.

D C♯dim C Cm
All your   life,

G/B   A7   D7sus   G
You were only wait - ing for this mo - ment to arise.

C   G/B   A7   D7sus   G
You were on - ly wait - ing for this mo - ment to arise.

C   G/B   A7   D7sus   G
You were on - ly waiting__ for this mo - ment to arise.

Blue Jay Way

Words and Music by
George Harrison

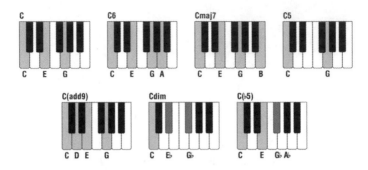

Intro		|C |C6 Cmaj7|C5 Cmaj7|

Intro |C | |C6 Cmaj7|C5 Cmaj7|

        | C6 Cmaj7 C(add9)|C Cmaj7|C |

Verse 1

 N.C.   C
 There's a fog upon L.A.,

 Cdim○   C
 And my friends have lost their way.

 Cdim○   C(♭5)
 We'll be over soon, they said,

 Cdim○   C
 Now they've lost themselves in-stead.

Chorus 1

 C6 Cmaj7 C5 Cmaj7
 Please don't be long,

 C6 Cmaj7 C5 Cmaj7
 Please don't you be very long,

 C6 Cmaj7 C5 Cmaj7
 Please don't be long,

 C6 C5 Cmaj7 C6 C5 C
 Or I may be a - sleep.

Copyright © 1967 Sony/ATV Music Publishing LLC
Copyright Renewed
All Rights Administered by Sony/ATV Music Publishing LLC, 8 Music Square West, Nashville, TN 37203
International Copyright Secured All Rights Reserved

Verse 2	**N.C.** **C** Well, it only goes to show,

Cdimo   **C**
And I told them where to go:

Cdimo   **C(♭5)**
Ask a policeman on the street,

Cdimo   **C**
There's so many there to meet.

Chorus 2   *Repeat Chorus 1*

Verse 3

N.C.   **C**
Now it's past my bed, I know, .

Cdimo   **C**
And I'd really like to go.

Cdimo   **C(♭5)**
Soon will be the break of day,

Cdimo   **C**
Sitting here in Blue Jay Way.

Chorus 3   *Repeat Chorus 1*

Chorus 4

C6   **Cmaj7 C5 Cmaj7**
Please don't   be   long,

C6   **Cmaj7**   **C5**   **Cmaj7**
Please don't you be very long,

C6   **Cmaj7 C5 Cmaj7**
Please don't   be   long.

Chorus 5   *Repeat Chorus 4*

Chorus 6   *Repeat Chorus 4*

Chorus 7

C
Don't be long, don't be long,

Don't be long, don't be long,

Don't be long, don't be long,

Don't be long.

Can't Buy Me Love

Words and Music by John Lennon
and Paul McCartney

Melody:

Can't buy me love, _____

Em   Am   Dm   G13

C7   F7   G7

Intro

            Em   Am   **Em   Am**
Can't buy me love, _____ love,

          Dm   G13
Can't buy me love.

Verse 1

        C7
I'll buy you a diamond ring, my friend,

If it makes you feel alright.

      F7
I'll get you anything, my friend,

      C7
If it makes you feel alright.

      G7   **F7**
'Cos I don't care too   much for money,

                   C7
(For) money can't buy me love.

Verse 2

        C7
I'll give you all I've got to give,

If you say you love me too.

    F7
I may not have a lot to give,

        C7
But what I've got I'll give to you.

G7   **F7**
I don't care too   much for money.

                 C7
(For) money can't buy me love.

Copyright © 1964 Sony/ATV Music Publishing LLC
Copyright Renewed
All Rights Administered by Sony/ATV Music Publishing LLC, 8 Music Square West, Nashville, TN 37203
International Copyright Secured   All Rights Reserved

Chorus 1

      Em Am
Can't buy me love,

C7
Everybody tells me so.

      Em Am
Can't buy me love,

Dm   **G13**
No, no, no, no.

Verse 3

C7
Say you don't need no diamond rings

And I'll be satisfied.

F7
Tell me that you want the kind of things

    C7
That money just can't buy.

G7   **F7**
I don't care too much for money.

        C7
For money can't buy me love.

Solo

C7				
F7		C7		
G7	F7	C7		

Chorus 2

Repeat Chorus 1

Verse 4

Repeat Verse 3

Outro

      Em Am   **Em Am**
Can't buy me love, _____ love,

      Dm G13
Can't buy me love.

C7
Oh.

Carry That Weight

Words and Music by John Lennon
and Paul McCartney

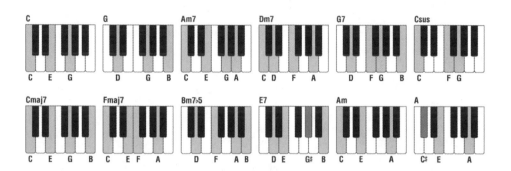

	C	**G**
Chorus 1	Boy, you're gonna carry that weight,	
		C
	Carry that weight a long time.	
		G
	Boy, you're gonna carry that weight,	
		C **G/B**
	Carry that weight a long time.	

Interlude | Am7 | Am7/D Dm7 | G7 | Csus C Cmaj7 |
             | Fmaj7 | Bm7♭5 E7 | Am | |

Copyright © 1969 Sony/ATV Songs LLC
Copyright Renewed
All Rights Administered by Sony/ATV Music Publishing, 8 Music Square West, Nashville, TN 37203
International Copyright Secured   All Rights Reserved

Verse

Am7   Am7/D Dm7

I never give you my pil - low,

G7   Csus C   Cmaj7

I only send you my in - vi - tations,

Fmaj7   Bm7♭5 E7   Am7   G C G

And in the middle of the cele - brations I break down.

Chorus 2

C   G

Boy, you're gonna carry that weight,

                    C

Carry that weight a long time.

                    G

Boy, you're gonna carry that weight,

                  C   G/B   A

Carry that weight a long time.

| C   G/B | A

Chains

Words and Music by Gerry Goffin
and Carole King

Chains,   my   ba - by's   got   me   locked up   in   chains, __

Intro | Bb | | | |

Verse 1
Bb
Chains,

My baby's got me locked up in chains,
                    Eb9   **Bb**
And they ain't the kind that you can see.
          F9   **Eb9**   **Bb**   **F**
Whoa, these chains of love__ got a hold on me. Yeah.

Verse 2
Bb
Chains,

Well, I can't break away from these chains.
          Eb9   **Bb**
Can't run around, 'cause I'm not free.
              F9   **Eb9**   **Bb**   **Bb7**
Whoa, these chains of love__ won't let me be, yeah.

© 1962 (Renewed 1990) SCREEN GEMS-EMI MUSIC INC.
All Rights Reserved   International Copyright Secured   Used by Permission

Bridge 1

Eb9
    I wanna tell you, pretty baby,

Bb   Bb7
    I think you're fine.

Eb9
    I'd like to love you,

    F
But, darling, I'm imprisoned by these...

Verse 3

Bb
Chains,

My baby's got me locked up in chains,

            Eb9   Bb
And they ain't the kind that you can see.

           F9   Eb9   Bb   F
Whoa, these chains of love__ got a hold on me. Yeah.

Bridge 2

Eb9
    Please believe me when I tell you

Bb   Bb7
    Your lips are sweet.

Eb9
    I'd like to kiss them,

    F
But I can't break away from all these...

Verse 4

Repeat Verse 1

Outro

Bb
Chains,

Chains of love.

Chains of love.

        Eb   Ebm
Chains of love.   *Fade out*

Come Together

Words and Music by John Lennon
and Paul McCartney

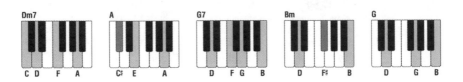

Intro ‖: **Dm7** | :‖
(Shoot me.) (Shoot me.)

Verse 1

Dm7
Here come old flat top, he come grooving up slowly,

He got joo joo eyeball, he one holy roller,

A
He got   hair down to his knees,

G7 N.C.
Got to be a joker, he just do what he please.

| **Dm7** | | | |

Verse 2

Dm7
He wear no shoe shine, he got toe jam football,

He got monkey finger, he shoot Coca Cola,

A
He say, "I know you, you know me.

G7 N.C.
One thing I can tell you is you got to be free."

Copyright © 1969 Sony/ATV Music Publishing LLC
Copyright Renewed
All Rights Administered by Sony/ATV Music Publishing LLC, 8 Music Square West, Nashville, TN 37203
International Copyright Secured   All Rights Reserved

Chorus 1	**Bm** Come to-gether,
	Bm/A G A Right now,
	N.C. Over me.
	|**Dm7** | | | |
Verse 3	**Dm7** He bag production, he got walrus gumboot,
	He got Ono sideboard, he one spinal cracker,
	A He got feet down below his knee,
	G7 N.C. Hold you in his armchair, you can feel his disease.
Chorus 2	**Bm** Come to-gether,
	Bm/A G A Right now,
	N.C. Over me.

Solo | **Dm7** | | | |
Right!   Come.

| **A** | | | **Dm7** | |
Come.

Verse 4
Dm7
He roller coaster, he got early warning,

He got muddy water, he one mojo filter,

A
He say,   "One and one and one is three."

G7 N.C.
Got to be good looking 'cause he's so hard to see.

Chorus 3
Bm
Come to-gether,

Bm/A G   A
Right   now,

N.C.
Over

Outro | **Dm7** | | | | | |
me.   Oh!

‖: Come together, yeah! :‖   *Repeat and fade*

A Day in the Life

Words and Music by John Lennon
and Paul McCartney

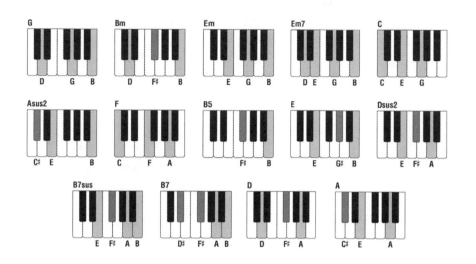

Intro

|G   Bm |Em Em7| C | | |

Verse 1

G   Bm   Em Em7
I read the news today, oh boy,

C   C/B   Asus2
About a lucky man who made the grade.

G   Bm   Em Em7
And though the news was rather sad,

C   F   Em Em7
Well, I just had to laugh,

C   F   Em   C
I saw the photograph.

Copyright © 1967 Sony/ATV Music Publishing LLC
Copyright Renewed
All Rights Administered by Sony/ATV Music Publishing LLC, 8 Music Square West, Nashville, TN 37203
International Copyright Secured   All Rights Reserved

Verse 2

```
G           Bm            Em   Em7
He blew his mind out in a car,

C       C/B         Asus2
He didn't notice that the lights had changed.

G           Bm              Em   Em7
A crowd of people stood and stared,

C               F
They'd seen his face before,
```

Em
Nobody was really sure

```
Em7                    C
If he was from the House of Lords.
```

Verse 3

```
G      Bm            Em   Em7
I saw a film today, oh boy,

C           C/B         Asus2
The English army had just won the war.

G           Bm              Em   Em7
A crowd of people turned a-way,

C       F          Em
But I just had to look,

    Em7      C
Having read the book,

        N.C.(B5)
I'd love to turn you on.
```

Interlude 1   ‖: N.C. | | | | :‖ E | |

Bridge

```
      E                                            Dsus2
Woke up, got out of bed, dragged a comb across my head,

              E                    B7sus
Found my way downstairs and drank a cup

          E            B7sus           B7
And looking up I noticed I was late.   Ha, ha, ha.

              E
Found my coat and grabbed my hat,

                       Dsus2
Made the bus in seconds flat,

          E                    B7sus
Found my way upstairs and had a smoke

          E                          B7sus
And somebody spoke and I went into a dream.
```

Interlude 2

```
C   G    D   A    E        C   G   D   A  |E D C D|
Ah, ___  ah, ___  ah, ___  ah, ___ ah. ___
```

Verse 4

```
G          Bm         Em  Em7
 I read the news today, oh boy,

C              C/B             Asus2
 Four thousand holes in Blackburn, Lancashire.

G            Bm            Em  Em7
 And though the holes were rather small,

C            F
 They had to count them all;

Em                              Em7                C
Now they know how many holes it takes to fill the Albert Hall.

              N.C.(B5)
I'd love to turn you on.
```

Outro

```
‖: N.C. |      |       |        |     :‖ E
```

The Continuing Story of Bungalow Bill

Words and Music by John Lennon
and Paul McCartney

Melody:

Hey, Bun-ga-low Bill, ___ what did you kill, ___

Em(add9) — E F#G B

C — C E G

G — D G B

Fm — C F A♭

G7 — D F G B

A — C# E A

E — E G# B

Dm — D F A

Am — C E A

F — C F A

Intro |Em(add9)| | | |

Chorus 1

C   G   C
Hey, Bungalow Bill,

Fm   C
What did you kill,

Fm   G
Bungalow Bill?

A   E   A
Hey, Bungalow Bill,

Dm   A
What did you kill,

Dm   E
Bungalow Bill?

Verse 1

         Am   Am/C   F   G
He went out tiger hunting, with his elephant and gun.

Am   Am/C   F   G
 In case of accidents, he always took his mom.

          E   G   Am   Fm
He's the all-American, bullet-headed, Saxon mother's son.

N.C.
(All the children sing!)

Copyright © 1968 Sony/ATV Music Publishing LLC
Copyright Renewed
All Rights Administered by Sony/ATV Music Publishing LLC, 8 Music Square West, Nashville, TN 37203
International Copyright Secured   All Rights Reserved

Chorus 2	*Repeat Chorus 1*

Verse 2

Am   Am/C   F   G
Deep in the jungle, where the mighty tiger lies,

Am   Am/C   F   G
Bill and his elephants were taken by surprise.

E   G   Am   Fm
So Captain Marvel zapped him right between the eyes.

N.C.
(All the children sing!)

Chorus 3

C   G   C
Hey, Bungalow Bill,

Fm   C
What did you kill,

Fm   G
Bungalow Bill?

A   E   A
Hey, Bungalow Bill,

Dm   A
What did you kill,

Dm   E
Bungalow Bill?

Verse 3

Am   Am/C   F   G
The children asked him if to kill was not a sin:

Am   Am/C   F   G
"Not when he looks so fierce," his mommy butted in.

E   G   Am   Fm
If looks could kill, it would have been us instead of him.

N.C.
(All the children sing!)

Chorus 4	***Repeat Chorus 1 till fade***

Cry Baby Cry

Words and Music by John Lennon
and Paul McCartney

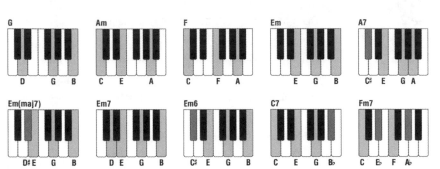

Intro

G   Am F   G
Cry baby cry,   make your mother sigh,

     Em   A7   F
She's old enough to know better.

Verse 1

     Em   Em(maj7)
The King of Marigold

         Em7
Was in the kitch-en

        Em6   C7 G
Cooking break-fast for the Queen.

     Em   Em(maj7)
The Queen was in the parlor,

     Em7
Playing piano

     Em6   C7
For the children of the King.

Copyright © 1968 Sony/ATV Music Publishing LLC
Copyright Renewed
All Rights Administered by Sony/ATV Music Publishing LLC, 8 Music Square West, Nashville, TN 37203
International Copyright Secured   All Rights Reserved

Chorus 1

```
G        Am F                    G
Cry baby cry,    make your mother sigh,

       Em                A7
She's old enough to know better.

     F     G
So cry baby cry.
```

Verse 2

```
         Em              Em(maj7)
The King was in the garden,

         Em7          Em6
Picking flowers for a friend

             C7  G
Who came to play.

       Em              Em(maj7)
The Queen was in the playroom,

         Em7
Painting pictures

         Em6          C7
For the children's holi-day.
```

Chorus 2

```
G        Am F                    G
Cry baby cry,    make your mother sigh,

       Em                A7
She's old enough to know better.

     F     G
So cry baby cry.
```

Verse 3

    Em   **Em(maj7)**
The Duchess of Kir-kaldy,

    Em7
Always smiling

    Em6   **C7** **G**
And ar-riving late for tea.

    Em   **Em(maj7)**
The Duke was having problems

     Em7
With a mes-sage

    Em6   **C7**
At the local Bird and Bee.

Chorus 3

G   **Am F**   **G**
Cry baby cry,   make your mother sigh,

    Em   **A7**
She's old enough to know better.

    F   **G**
So cry baby cry.

Verse 4

    Em   **Em(maj7)**
At twelve o'clock a meeting

    Em7
'Round the table

    Em6   **C7** **G**
For a seance in the dark.

    Em   **Em(maj7)**
With voices out of no-where,

    Em7
Put on specially

    Em6   **C7**
By the children, for a lark.

Chorus 4

<pre>
G   Am F   G
Cry Baby cry,   make your mother sigh,

    Em   A7
She's old enough to know better.

    F   G
So cry baby cry.

        Am   F   G
Cry, cry, cry baby,   make your mother sigh,

    Em   A7
She's old enough to know better,

    F   G
So cry baby cry.

        Am   F   G
Cry, cry, cry,   make your mother sigh,

    Em   A7
She's old enough to know better,

    F   G
So cry baby cry.
</pre>

Outro

<pre>
Fm7
Can you take me back where I came from,
</pre>

Can you take me back?

Can you take me back where I came from,

Brother, can you take me back,

Can you take me back?   *Fade out*

Day Tripper

Words and Music by John Lennon
and Paul McCartney

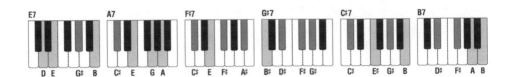

Intro | E7 | ‖: E7 | | | :‖

Verse 1

E7
Got a good reason

For taking the easy way out.

A7
Got a good reason

   E7
For taking the easy way out, now.

      F#7
She was a day tripper,

One way ticket, yeah.

      A7 G#7   **C#7**
It took me so   long to find out,

      B7
And I found out.

| E7 | | | | |

Verse 2

E7
She's a big teaser,

She took me half the way there.
A7
She's a big teaser,
E7
She took me half the way there, now.
     F#7
She was a day tripper,

One way ticket, yeah.
     A7 G#7   C#7
It took me so long to find out,
       B7
And I found out.

Solo

‖: B7 │   │   │   :‖ *Play 3 times*

│ E7 │   │   │   │

Verse 3

E7
Tried to please her,

She only played one night stands.
A7
Tried to please her,
E7
She only played one night stands, now.
     F#7
She was a day tripper,

Sunday driver, yeah.
     A7 G#7   C#7
It took me so long to find out,
       B7
And I found out.

Outro

‖: E7 │   │   │   :‖

‖: Day tripper, day tripper, yeah.

Day tripper, day tripper, yeah. :‖ *Repeat and fade*

Dear Prudence

Words and Music by John Lennon
and Paul McCartney

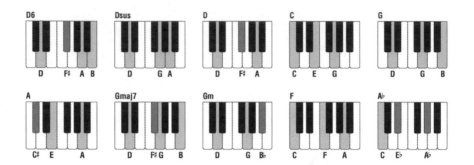

Intro

| D6 Dsus | D C/D | G/D A/D | C/D | |
| D D/C | Gmaj7/B Gm/B♭ | |

Verse 1

          D   D/C Gmaj7/B Gm/B♭
Dear   Prudence,

                    D D/C Gmaj7/B Gm/B♭
Won't you come out to play?

          D   D/C Gmaj7/B Gm/B♭
Dear   Prudence,

                    D D/C Gmaj7/B Gm/B♭
Greet the brand new day.

          D   D/C
The sun is up, the sky is blue,

     Gmaj7/B   Gm/B♭
It's beautiful and so are you,

          D   D/C
Dear Prudence,

     C   G   D D/C Gmaj7/B Gm/B♭
Won't you come out to play?

Copyright © 1968 Sony/ATV Music Publishing LLC
Copyright Renewed
All Rights Administered by Sony/ATV Music Publishing LLC, 8 Music Square West, Nashville, TN 37203
International Copyright Secured   All Rights Reserved

PIANO CHORD SONGBOOK

Verse 2

      D   **D/C** **Gmaj7/B** **Gm/B**♭
Dear Prudence,

        D **D/C** **Gmaj7/B** **Gm/B**♭
Open up your eyes.

      D   **D/C** **Gmaj7/B** **Gm/B**♭
Dear Prudence,

        D **D/C** **Gmaj7/B** **Gm/B**♭
See the sunny skies.

      D   **D/C**
The wind is low, the birds will sing,

   Gmaj7/B   **Gm/B**♭
That you are part of everything,

      D   **D/C**
Dear Prudence,

C   **G**   **D** **G/D** **A/D** **G/D**
Won't you open up your eyes?

Bridge

        D   **G/D**
Look a-round, 'round, ('Round, 'round, 'round,

A/D   **G/D**
'Round, 'round, 'round, 'round, 'round.)

        D   **G/D**
Look a-round, 'round, 'round, ('Round, 'round,

A/D   **G/D**
'Round, 'round, 'round, 'round, 'round.)

      F   **A**♭ **G**
Look a-round, ah.

|**D** **D/C** |**Gmaj7/B** **Gm/B**♭ |

Verse 3

        D   **D/C Gmaj7/B Gm/B♭**
Dear Prudence,

           D D/C Gmaj7/B Gm/B♭
Let me see you smile.

        D   **D/C Gmaj7/B Gm/B♭**
Dear Prudence,

          D D/C Gmaj7/B Gm/B♭
Like a little child.

        D   **D/C**
The clouds will be a daisy chain

   Gmaj7/B   **Gm/B♭**
So let me see you smile again,

        D   **D/C**
Dear Prudence,

C   **G**   **D D/C Gmaj7/B Gm/B♭**
Won't you let me see you smile?

Verse 4

        D   **D/C Gmaj7/B Gm/B♭**
Dear Prudence,

           D D/C Gmaj7/B Gm/B♭
Won't you come out to play?

        D   **D/C Gmaj7/B Gm/B♭**
Dear Prudence,

           D D/C Gmaj7/B Gm/B♭
Greet the brand new day.

        D   **D/C**
The sun is up, the sky is blue,

   Gmaj7/B   **Gm/B♭**
It's beautiful and so are you,

        D   **D/C**
Dear Prudence,

C   **G**   **D**
Won't you come out to play?

|**D6** **Dsus** |**D** **C/D** |**G/D** **A/D** |**C/D** |**D**

Dig a Pony

Words and Music by John Lennon
and Paul McCartney

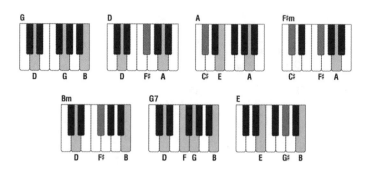

Intro   ‖: G |D |A | :‖

Verse 1
A   D/A A   D/A A   D/A A
I

    F#m
Dig a pony.

        Bm   G7
Well, you can celebrate anything you want,

      Bm   G7   E
Yes,   you can celebrate any-thing you want, oh!

Verse 2
A   D/A A   D/A A   D/A A
I

    F#m
Do a road hog.

        Bm   G7
Well, you can penetrate any place you go,

     Bm   G7   E
Yes,   you can penetrate any place you go, I told you so.

Copyright © 1970 Sony/ATV Music Publishing LLC
Copyright Renewed
All Rights Administered by Sony/ATV Music Publishing LLC, 8 Music Square West, Nashville, TN 37203
International Copyright Secured   All Rights Reserved

Chorus 1

<pre>
G   D   A
</pre>
All I want is you,

<pre>
G   D   A
</pre>
Everything has got to be just like you want it to.

N.C.
Because…

Verse 3

<pre>
A D/A A D/A A D/A A
</pre>
I

<pre>
      F♯m
</pre>
Pick a moondog.

<pre>
          Bm   G7
</pre>
Well, you can radiate everything you are,

<pre>
   Bm   G7   E
</pre>
Yes,   you can radiate every-thing you are, oh now.

Verse 4

<pre>
A D/A A D/A A D/A A
</pre>
I

<pre>
      F♯m
</pre>
Roll a stoney.

<pre>
          Bm   G7
</pre>
Well, you can imitate everyone you know,

<pre>
   Bm   G7   E
</pre>
Yes,   you can imitate every-one you know, I told you so.

| *Chorus 2* | *Repeat Chorus 1* |

Solo

```
|A  D/A |A  D/A |A  D/A |A  D/A |
|F#m    |       |Bm     |G7     |
|       |Bm     |G7     |E      |
```

Verse 5

A   D/A A   D/A A   D/A A
I

       F#m
Feel the wind blow.

      Bm   G7
Well, you can indicate everything you see,

   Bm   G7   E
Yes,   you can indicate anything you see, oh now.

Verse 6

A   D/A A   D/A A   D/A A
I,

       F#m
Cold and lonely.

      Bm   G7
Well, you can syndicate any boat you row,

   Bm   G7   E
Yeah,   you can syndicate any boat you row, I told you so.

| *Chorus 3* | *Repeat Chorus 1* |

Outro

```
||: G    |D     |A     |      :||
```

Do You Want to Know a Secret?

Words and Music by John Lennon
and Paul McCartney

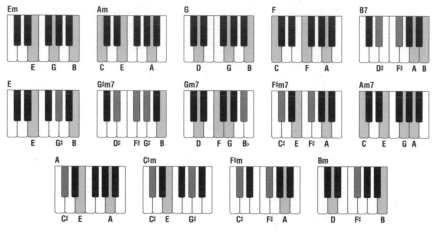

Intro

   Em
             Am Em
You'll never know how much I really love you,

G   F B7
You'll never know how much I really care.

Verse 1

E G#m7 Gm7 F#m7
Listen,

   B7   E G#m7 Gm7 F#m7
Do you want to know a secret?

   B7   E
Do you promise not to tell?

G#m7 Gm7 F#m7 Am7
  Woh, oh, oh.

E G#m7 Gm7 F#m7
Closer,

   B7   E G#m7 Gm7 F#m7
Let me whisper in your ear,

   B7   A
Say the words you long to hear,

B7   C#m/G# F#m7 B7
 I'm in love with you, woo, oo, oo, oo.

© 1963 NORTHERN SONGS LTD. (UK)
Copyright Renewed
All Rights in the U.S. and Canada Controlled by EMI UNART CATALOG INC. (Publishing) and ALFRED PUBLISHING CO., INC. (Print)
All Rights Reserved   Used by Permission

Verse 2   *Repeat Verse 1*

Bridge

A   F#m   C#m   Bm
I've known a secret for a week or two,

A   F#m
Nobody knows,

C#m   Bm F#m B7
Just we two.

Verse 3

E   G#m7 Gm7 F#m7
Listen,

     B7   E   G#m7 Gm7 F#m7
Do you want to know a secret?

     B7   E
Do you promise not to tell?

G#m7 Gm7 F#m7 Am7
    Woh, oh,   oh.

E   G#m7 Gm7 F#m7
Closer,

     B7   E   G#m7 Gm7 F#m7
Let me whisper in your ear,

     B7   A
Say the words you long to hear,

B7   C#m/G#   F#m7 B7
  I'm in love with you, woo, oo, oo,   oo.

  C#m/G#   F#m7 B7
‖: Woo, oo, oo,   oo. :‖ *Repeat and fade*

Doctor Robert

Words and Music by John Lennon
and Paul McCartney

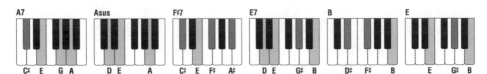

Ring my   friend, _ I   said __ you'd call,   Doc - tor   Rob-ert.

Intro |A7 Asus |A7 Asus |A7 Asus |A7 Asus |

Verse 1

A7
Ring my friend, I said you'd call, Doctor Robert.

Day or night, he'll be there any time at all, Doctor Robert.
F#7
Doctor Robert, you're a new and better man,

He helps you to understand,
E7   F#7   B
He does everything he can, Doctor Robert.

Verse 2

A7
If you're down, he'll pick you up, Doctor Robert.

Take a drink from his special cup, Doctor Robert.
F#7
Doctor Robert, he's a man you must believe,

Helping anyone in need,
E7   F#7   B
No one can suc-ceed like Doctor Robert.

Copyright © 1966 Sony/ATV Music Publishing LLC
Copyright Renewed
All Rights Administered by Sony/ATV Music Publishing LLC, 8 Music Square West, Nashville, TN 37203
International Copyright Secured   All Rights Reserved

Bridge 1	**B** **E/B** **B** Well, well, well, you're feeling fine, **E/B** Well, well, well, he'll make you, **A7** Doctor Robert.

Bridge 1

     B   **E/B**   **B**
Well, well, well, you're feeling fine,

                       E/B
Well, well, well, he'll make you,

    A7
Doctor Robert.

Verse 3

A7
My friend works for the National Health, Doctor Robert.

You'll pay money just to see yourself with Doctor Robert.
    F♯7
Doctor Robert, you're a new and better man,

He helps you to understand,
        E7   **F♯7**   **B**
He does everything he can, Doc Robert.

Bridge 2

Repeat Bridge 1

Outro

A7
Ring my friend, I said you'd call,

Doctor Robert.

Ring my friend, I said you'd call,

Doc Robert.
    F♯7
Doctor Robert!   *Fade out*

Don't Bother Me

Words and Music by
George Harrison

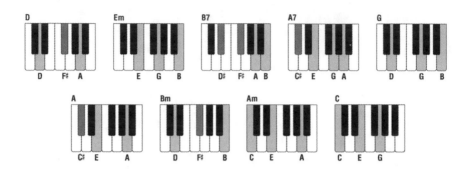

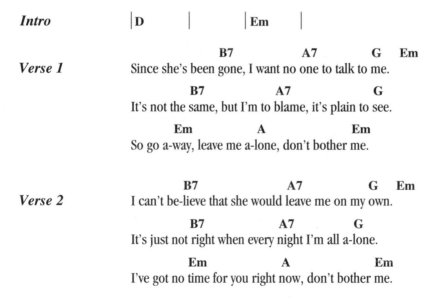

Intro | D | | Em |

Verse 1

                  B7   **A7**   **G**   **Em**
Since she's been gone, I want no one to talk to me.

            B7   **A7**   **G**
It's not the same, but I'm to blame, it's plain to see.

         Em   **A**   **Em**
So go a-way, leave me a-lone, don't bother me.

Verse 2

          B7   **A7**   **G**   **Em**
I can't be-lieve that she would leave me on my own.

         B7   **A7**   **G**
It's just not right when every night I'm all a-lone.

          Em   **A**   **Em**
I've got no time for you right now, don't bother me.

Copyright © 1963 UNIVERSAL/DICK JAMES MUSIC LTD.
Copyright Renewed
All Rights for the U.S. and Canada Controlled and Administered by UNIVERSAL - SONGS OF POLYGRAM INTERNATIONAL, INC.
All Rights Reserved   Used by Permission

Bridge 1	D Em I know I'll never be the same

Bridge 1

           D   Em
I know I'll never be the same

           D   Em
If I don't get her back again,

            Bm   Am
Because I know she'll always be

         C   Em
The only girl for me.

Verse 3

          B7   A7   G   Em
But till she's here, please don't come near, just stay away.

          B7   A7   G
I'll let you know when she's come home, until that day,

           Em   A   Em
Don't come a-round, leave me a-lone, don't bother me.

Interlude

| B7 | A7 | G | Em | |
| B7 | A7 | G | | |

N.C.   Em   A   Em
I've got no time for you right now, don't bother me.

Bridge 2   *Repeat Bridge 1*

Verse 4

N.C.   B7   A7   G   Em
But till she's here, please don't come near, just stay away.

          B7   A7   G
I'll let you know when she's come home, until that day,

           Em   A   Em
Don't come a-round, leave me a-lone, don't bother me.

     A   Em
‖: Don't bother me. :‖ *Repeat and fade*

Don't Let Me Down

Words and Music by John Lennon
and Paul McCartney

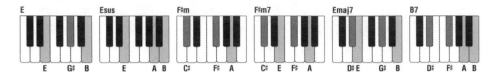

Intro

|E Esus |E |

Chorus 1

F♯m
Don't let me down.

E Esus E
Don't let me down.

F♯m
Don't let me down,

E Esus E
Don't let me down.

Verse 1

N.C.   F♯m7
Nobody ever loved me like she does,

Emaj7 Esus E
Ooh, she does, yes she does,

N.C.   F♯m7
And if somebody loved me like she do me,

Emaj7 Esus E
Ooh, she do me, yes she does.

Chorus 2

Repeat Chorus 1

Copyright © 1969 Sony/ATV Music Publishing LLC
Copyright Renewed
All Rights Administered by Sony/ATV Music Publishing LLC, 8 Music Square West, Nashville, TN 37203
International Copyright Secured   All Rights Reserved

Bridge

N.C.   E

I'm in love for the first time,

                              B7

Don't you know it's going to last.

It's a love that lasts forever,

                  E   **Esus**   **E**

It's a love that has no   past.

Chorus 3   *Repeat Chorus 1*

Verse 2

N.C.   **F♯m7**

And from the first time that she really done me,

                         Emaj7   **Esus**   **E**

Ooh, she done me, she done me good.

N.C.   **F♯m7**

I guess nobody ever really done me,

                         Emaj7   **Esus**   **E**

Ooh, she done me, she done me good.

Chorus 4

              F♯m

Don't let me down, hey!

             E   **Esus**   **E**

Don't let me down.

              F♯m

Don't let me down,

             E   **Esus**   **E**

Don't let me down.

F♯m   **E**   **Esus**   **E**

  Don't let me down,

             F♯m

Don't let me down.

Can you dig it?

             E   **Esus**   **E**

Don't let me down.

Don't Pass Me By

Words and Music by
Richard Starkey

Intro | C | |

Verse 1

    C
I listen for your footsteps coming up the drive,

F
Listen for your footsteps, but they don't arrive.

G
Waiting for your knock, dear, on my old front door,

    F
I don't hear it,

                      C
Does it mean you don't love me any-more?

Verse 2

    C
I hear the clock a ticking on the mantel shelf,

F
See the hands a moving, but I'm by myself.

    G
I wonder where you are tonight and why I'm by myself,

    F
I don't see you,

                      C
Does it mean you don't love me any-more?

Copyright © 1968 STARTLING MUSIC LTD.
Copyright Renewed
International Copyright Secured   All Rights Reserved

Chorus 1

                          C
Don't pass me by, don't make me cry,

Don't make me blue,

                  F
'Cause you know, darling, I love only you.

                 C
You'll never know it hurt me so, I hate to see you go,

                G   **F**   **C**
Don't pass me by, don't make me cry.

Verse 3

               C
I'm sorry that I doubted you, I was so unfair,

F
You were in a car crash and you lost your hair.

        G
You said that you would be late, about an hour or two,

        F
I say that's alright,

                                C
I'm waiting here, just waiting to hear from you.

Chorus 2

                          C
Don't pass me by, don't make me cry,

Don't make me blue,

                  F
'Cause you know, darling, I love only you.

                 C
You'll never know it hurt me so, I hate to see you go,

                G   **F**
Don't pass me by, don't make me cry.

Interlude | C | | *Drums for 2 bars* | C | |

Chorus 3   *Repeat Chorus 2*

Outro | C | | F | G | Dm7 C

Drive My Car

Words and Music by John Lennon
and Paul McCartney

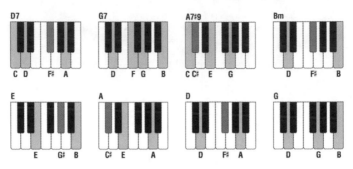

Intro | D7 | |

Verse 1

D7   G7
Asked a girl what she wanted to be,

D7   G7
She said, baby, can't you see?

D7   G7
I wanna be famous, a star of the screen,

   A7#9
But you can do something in between.

Chorus 1

Bm   G7 Bm   G7
Baby, you can drive my car, yes I'm gonna be a star,

Bm   E   A   D   G A
Baby, you can drive my car, and maybe I'll love you.

Verse 2

D7   G7
I told that girl that my prospects were good,

D7   G7
She said, baby, it's understood.

D7   G7
Working for peanuts is all very fine,

   A7#9
But I can show you a better time.

Copyright © 1965 Sony/ATV Music Publishing LLC
Copyright Renewed
All Rights Administered by Sony/ATV Music Publishing LLC, 8 Music Square West, Nashville, TN 37203
International Copyright Secured   All Rights Reserved

Chorus 2

Bm   G7   Bm   G7
Baby, you can drive my car, yes I'm gonna be a star,

Bm   E   A   D   G
Baby, you can drive my car, and maybe I'll love you.

A N.C.
    Beep, beep, mm, beep, beep, yeah!

Solo

| D7 | G7 | D7 | G7 | |
| D7 | G7 | A | | |

Chorus 3   *Repeat Chorus 1*

Verse 3

D7   G7
   I told that girl I could start right away,

D7   G7
   And she said, listen, babe, I've got something to say,

D7   G7
   I've got no car, and it's breaking my heart,

   A7$\sharp$9
But I've found a driver, and that's a start.

Chorus 4

Bm   G7   Bm   G7
Baby, you can drive my car, yes I'm gonna be a star,

Bm   E   A   D   G
Baby, you can drive my car, and maybe I'll love you.

A N.C.   D   G
   Beep, beep, mm, beep, beep, yeah!

    A   D   G
$\|$:   Beep, beep, mm, beep, beep, yeah!   :$\|$ *Repeat and fade*

Eight Days a Week

Words and Music by John Lennon
and Paul McCartney

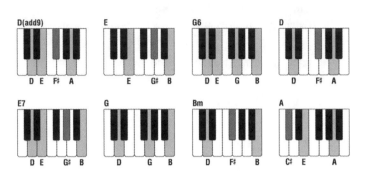

Intro | D(add9) | E | G6 | D(add9) |

Verse 1

    D   **E7**
Ooh, I need your love, babe,

    G   **D**
Guess you know it's true.

                  E7
Hope you need my love, babe,

    G   **D**
Just like I need you.

Chorus 1

    Bm   **G**
Hold me, love me.

    Bm   **E**
Hold me, love me.

      D   **E7**
I ain't got nothing but love, babe,

    G   **D**
  Eight days a week.

Copyright © 1964 Sony/ATV Music Publishing LLC
Copyright Renewed
All Rights Administered by Sony/ATV Music Publishing LLC, 8 Music Square West, Nashville, TN 37203
International Copyright Secured   All Rights Reserved

Verse 2

```
D              E7
Love you every day, girl,

        G         D
You're always on my mind.

D              E7
One thing I can say, girl,

G              D
Love you all the time.
```

Chorus 2   *Repeat Chorus 1*

Bridge 1

```
A
Eight days a week,

 Bm
I love you.

E
Eight days a week

 G      A
Is not enough to show I care.
```

Verse 3   *Repeat Verse 1*

Chorus 3   *Repeat Chorus 1*

Bridge 2   *Repeat Bridge 1*

Verse 4   *Repeat Verse 2*

Chorus 4

```
Bm    G
Hold me, love me.

Bm    E
Hold me, love me.

D         E7
I ain't got nothing but love, girl,

G      D
  Eight days a week.

G      D
  Eight days a week.

G      D
  Eight days a week.
```

Outro |Dadd9 |E |G6 |Dadd9

Eleanor Rigby

Words and Music by John Lennon
and Paul McCartney

Melody:

Ah, _____ look at all _____ the lone - ly peo - ple!

Intro

    C   Em
Ah, look at all the lonely people!
    C   Em
Ah, look at all the lonely people!

Verse 1

    Em
Eleanor Rigby,

                                          C
Picks up the rice in the church where a wedding has been,

              Em
Lives in a dream.

Waits at the window,

                            Em7   C
Wearing a face that she keeps in a jar by the door,

              Em
Who is it for?

Chorus 1

    Em7   Em6   Em(add♭6)   Em
All the lonely people, where do they all come from?
    Em7   Em6   Em(add♭6)   Em
All the lonely people, where do they all be-long?

Copyright © 1966 Sony/ATV Music Publishing LLC
Copyright Renewed
All Rights Administered by Sony/ATV Music Publishing LLC, 8 Music Square West, Nashville, TN 37203
International Copyright Secured   All Rights Reserved

Verse 2	**Em** Father McKenzie,

Em

Verse 2 Father McKenzie,

                                           C

Writing the words of a sermon that no one will hear,

                  Em

No one comes near.

Look at him working,

                                       C

Darning his socks in the night when there's nobody there,

                  Em

What does he care?

Chorus 2 *Repeat Chorus 1*

           C   **Em**

Bridge Ah, look at all the lonely people!

           C   **Em**

Ah, look at all the lonely people!

           Em

Verse 3 Eleanor Rigby,

                                         C

Died in the church and was buried along with her name,

                  Em

Nobody came.

Father McKenzie,

                                         C

Wiping the dirt from his hands as he walks from the grave,

                  Em

No one was saved.

Chorus 3 *Repeat Chorus 1*

The End

Words and Music by John Lennon
and Paul McCartney

Melody:

Oh,   yeah!   All   right!

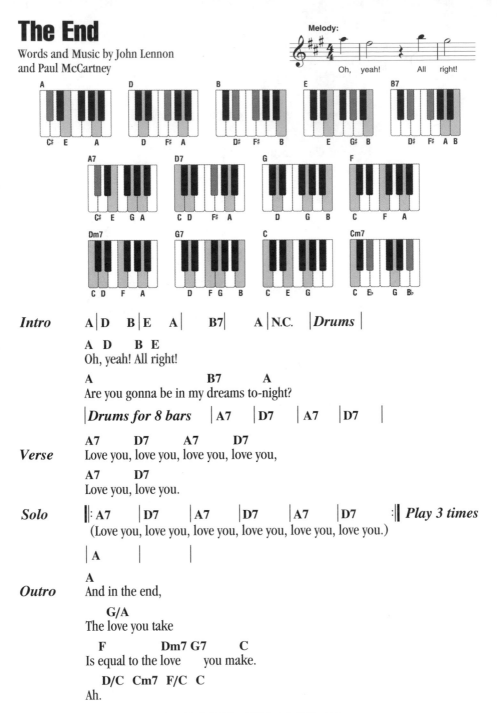

Intro   A | D   B | E   A | B7 | A | N.C. | *Drums* |

A   D   B   E
Oh, yeah! All right!

A   B7   A
Are you gonna be in my dreams to-night?

| *Drums for 8 bars* | A7 | D7 | A7 | D7 |

A7   D7   A7   D7
Verse   Love you, love you, love you, love you,

A7   D7
Love you, love you.

Solo   ‖: A7 | D7 | A7 | D7 | A7 | D7   :‖ *Play 3 times*
(Love you, love you, love you, love you, love you, love you.)

| A | | |

A
Outro   And in the end,

    G/A
The love you take

    F   Dm7 G7   C
Is equal to the love   you make.

    D/C   Cm7   F/C   C
Ah.

Copyright © 1969 Sony/ATV Music Publishing LLC
Copyright Renewed
All Rights Administered by Sony/ATV Music Publishing LLC, 8 Music Square West, Nashville, TN 37203
International Copyright Secured   All Rights Reserved

PIANO CHORD SONGBOOK

Everybody's Got Something to Hide Except Me and My Monkey

Words and Music by John Lennon
and Paul McCartney

Come on, come on, ___   come on, come on. ___

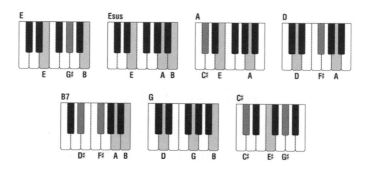

Intro	‖: E Esus A │ E Esus A :‖
Verse 1	**E** Come on, come on,
	Come on, come on.
	Come on is such a joy,
	Come on is such a joy.
	Come on is take it easy,
	Come on is take it easy.

Copyright © 1968 Sony/ATV Music Publishing LLC
Copyright Renewed
All Rights Administered by Sony/ATV Music Publishing LLC, 8 Music Square West, Nashville, TN 37203
International Copyright Secured   All Rights Reserved

Chorus 1

     A
Take it easy,

     D
Take it easy.

     B7
Every-body's got something to hide

                 E   **D G E G D**
Except for me and my monkey.

Verse 2

     E
The deeper you go, the higher you fly,

The higher you fly, the deeper you go,

So come on, come on.

Come on is such a joy,

Come on is such a joy.

Come on is make it easy,

Come on is take it easy.

Chorus 2   *Repeat Chorus 1*

Verse 3

E
Your inside is out when your outside is in,

Your outside is in when your inside is out,

So come on, come on,

Come on is such a joy,

Come on is such a joy.

Come on is make it easy,

Come on is make it easy.

Chorus 3

A
Make it easy,

D
Make it easy.

B7
Every-body's got something to hide

E   D G E G D
Except for me and my monkey.

Outro

N.C.
(Come on, come on, come on.)

| C♯ D C♯ D | C♯ D C♯ D | C♯ D C♯ D |

‖: E Esus A | E Esus A :‖ *Repeat and fade*
(Come on, come on, come on.)

Every Little Thing

Words and Music by John Lennon
and Paul McCartney

Melody:

When I'm walk-ing be - side her,

A   C♯ E   A

D   D F♯ A

E   E G♯ B

G   D G B

Bm   D F♯ B

Intro |A |D   E |

Verse 1

     A   D   E
     When I'm walking be-side her,

     A   G   D
     People tell me I'm luck-y,

     Bm   Bm/A   E/G♯ A
     Yes, I know I'm a lucky guy.

                 D   E
     I remember the first time

     A   G   D
     I was lonely with-out her,

     Bm   Bm/A   E/G♯   A
     Yes, I'm thinking a-bout her now.

Chorus 1

     A   G
     Every little thing she does,

         G/A   A G/A   A
     She does for me,   yeah,

            G
     And you know the things she does,

         G/A   A G/A   A
     She does for me,   ooh.

Copyright © 1964 Sony/ATV Music Publishing LLC
Copyright Renewed
All Rights Administered by Sony/ATV Music Publishing LLC, 8 Music Square West, Nashville, TN 37203
International Copyright Secured   All Rights Reserved

Verse 2

<pre>
A   D   E
When I'm with her I'm hap-py,

A   G   D
Just to know that she loves me,

Bm   Bm/A   E/G♯   A
Yes, I know that she loves me now.

                    D   E
There is one thing I'm sure of,

A   G D
I will love her for-ev-er,

Bm   Bm/A   E/G♯ A
For I know love will never die.
</pre>

Chorus 2   *Repeat Chorus 1*

Solo |A |D E |A |G D |Bm Bm/A |E/G♯ A |

Chorus 3   *Repeat Chorus 1*

Outro

<pre>
     A D E
||:   Every little thing. :|| *Repeat and fade*
</pre>

Fixing a Hole

Words and Music by John Lennon
and Paul McCartney

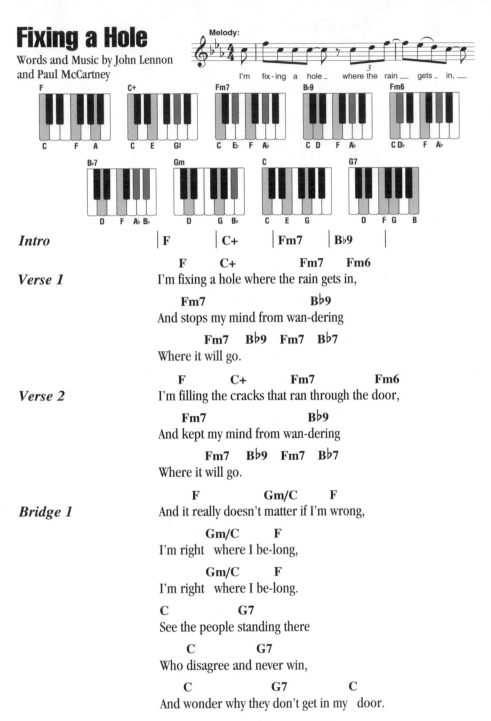

Intro

| F | C+ | Fm7 | Bb9 | |

Verse 1

    F   C+   Fm7   Fm6
I'm fixing a hole where the rain gets in,

    Fm7   Bb9
And stops my mind from wan-dering

      Fm7   Bb9 Fm7 Bb7
Where it will go.

Verse 2

      F   C+   Fm7   Fm6
I'm filling the cracks that ran through the door,

    Fm7   Bb9
And kept my mind from wan-dering

      Fm7   Bb9 Fm7 Bb7
Where it will go.

Bridge 1

      F   Gm/C   F
And it really doesn't matter if I'm wrong,

      Gm/C   F
I'm right   where I be-long,

      Gm/C   F
I'm right   where I be-long.

C   G7
See the people standing there

    C   G7
Who disagree and never win,

    C   G7   C
And wonder why they don't get in my door.

Copyright © 1967 Sony/ATV Music Publishing LLC
Copyright Renewed
All Rights Administered by Sony/ATV Music Publishing LLC, 8 Music Square West, Nashville, TN 37203
International Copyright Secured   All Rights Reserved

Verse 3

      F   **C+**   **Fm7**   **Fm6**
I'm painting the room in a col-orful way,
     Fm7   **Bb9**
And when my mind is wan-dering,
      Fm7   **Bb9**
There I will go,
Fm7   **Bb7**
Ooh, ooh, uh, uh,   hey, hey, hey.

Solo

| F   C+ | Fm7 Fm6 | Fm7 | Bb9 |
| Fm7 | Bb9 | Fm7 | Bb9 |

Bridge 2

        F   **Gm/C**   **F**
And it really doesn't matter if I'm wrong,
      Gm/C   **F**
I'm right   where I be-long,
      Gm/C   **F**
I'm right   where I be-long.
C   **G7**
Silly people run around,
    C   **G7**
They worry me and never ask me
C   **G7**   **C**
Why they don't get past my door.

Verse 4

      F   **C+**   **Fm7**   **Fm6**
I'm taking the time for a number of things
    Fm7   **Bb9**
That weren't important yesterday,
     Fm7 **Bb9** **Fm7** **Bb7**
And I still go.

Verse 5

      F   **C+**   **Fm7**   **Fm6**
‖: I'm fixing a hole where the rain gets in,
    Fm7   **Bb9**
And stops my mind from wandering
    Fm7 **Bb9**
Where it will go,
    Fm7 **Bb7**
Where it will go.   :‖   *Repeat and fade*

The Fool on the Hill

Words and Music by John Lennon
and Paul McCartney

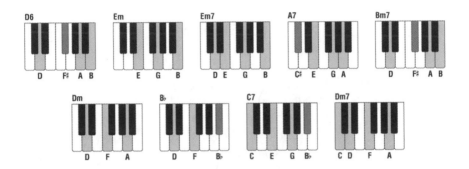

Intro | D6 | |

Verse 1

    D6   Em/D
Day after day, a-lone on a hill,

        D6   Em/D
The man with the foolish grin is keeping perfectly still.

        Em7   A7
But nobody wants to know him,

           D6   Bm7
They can see that he's just a fool.

       Em7   A7
And he never gives an an-swer;

Copyright © 1967 Sony/ATV Music Publishing LLC
Copyright Renewed
All Rights Administered by Sony/ATV Music Publishing LLC, 8 Music Square West, Nashville, TN 37203
International Copyright Secured   All Rights Reserved

Chorus 1

           Dm B♭/D   Dm
But the fool   on the hill

       B♭/D
Sees the sun going down,

       C7
And the eyes in his head

         Dm   **Dm7 D6**
See the world spinning 'round.

Verse 2

D6   **Em/D**
Well on the way, his head in a cloud,

    D6   **Em/D**
The man of a thousand voices talking perfectly loud.

    Em7   **A7**
But nobody ever hears him,

       D6   **Bm7**
Or the sound he appears to make.

    Em7   **A7**
And he never seems to no-tice;

Chorus 2   *Repeat Chorus 1*

Solo   ‖: **D6** | | **Em/D** | :‖

Verse 3

    Em7   **A7**
And nobody seems to like him,

       D6   **Bm7**
They can tell what he wants to do.

    Em7   **A7**
And he never shows his feelings;

Chorus 3

        Dm Bb/D Dm
But the fool   on the hill

      Bb/D
Sees the sun going down,

    C7
And the eyes in his head

      Dm   **Dm7 D6**
See the world spinning 'round.

D6   **Em/D**
 (Oh,   oh,

D6   **Em/D**
'Round, 'round, 'round, 'round, 'round.)

Verse 4

    Em7   **A7**
And he never listens to them,

    D6   **Bm7**
He knows that they're the fool.

Em7   **A7**
 They don't like him;

Chorus 4

    Dm
The fool on the hill

Sees the sun going down,

    C7
And the eyes in his head

      Dm   **Dm7**
See the world spinning 'round.

 D6
‖: (Oh,

Em7/D
'Round, 'round, 'round,

'Round, and…) :‖ *Repeat and fade*

Get Back

Words and Music by John Lennon
and Paul McCartney

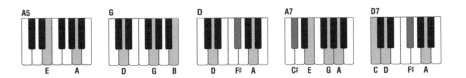

Intro | A5 | | | G D/A |

Verse 1

A5
Jo-Jo was a man who thought he was a loner,

D   A5
But he knew it couldn't last.

Jo-Jo left his home in Tucson, Arizona

D   A5
For some California grass.

Chorus 1

A7
Get back, get back,

D7   A5   G   D/A
Get back to where you once belonged.

A7
Get back, get back,

D7   A5
Get back to where you once belonged.

Get back, Jo-Jo.

Copyright © 1969 Sony/ATV Music Publishing LLC
Copyright Renewed
All Rights Administered by Sony/ATV Music Publishing LLC, 8 Music Square West, Nashville, TN 37203
International Copyright Secured   All Rights Reserved

| *Solo 1* | ‖: A5 | | |D | |A5 G D/A :‖ |

Chorus 2

A7
Get back, get back,

D7   A5   G   D/A
Get back to where you once belonged.

A7
Get back, get back,

A5   D
Get back to where you once belonged.

A5
Get back, Jo-Jo.

Solo 2   *Repeat Solo 1*

Verse 2

A5
Sweet Loretta Martin though she was a woman,

D   A5
But she was another man.

All the girls around her say she's got it coming

D   A5
But she gets it while she can.

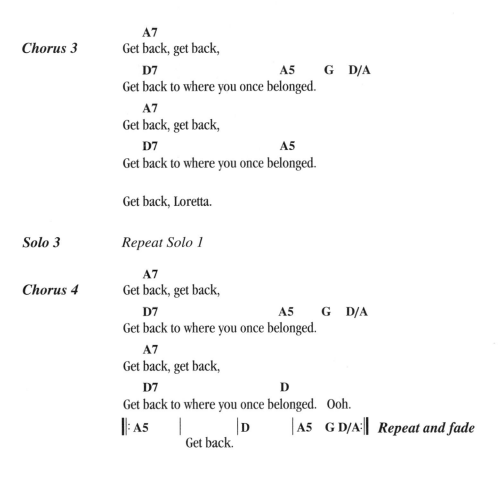

Chorus 3

A7
Get back, get back,

D7   A5   G   D/A
Get back to where you once belonged.

A7
Get back, get back,

D7   A5
Get back to where you once belonged.

Get back, Loretta.

Solo 3   *Repeat Solo 1*

Chorus 4

A7
Get back, get back,

D7   A5   G   D/A
Get back to where you once belonged.

A7
Get back, get back,

D7   D
Get back to where you once belonged.   Ooh.

‖: A5 | |D |A5   G D/A:‖ *Repeat and fade*
          Get back.

For No One

Words and Music by John Lennon
and Paul McCartney

Melody:

Your day _ breaks,   your mind _ aches,

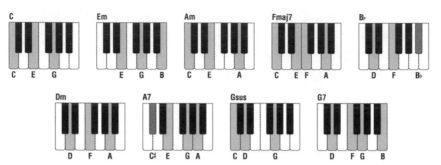

Verse 1

    C   Em/B
Your day breaks,   your mind aches,

Am   C/G
You find that all her words

   Fmaj7   Bb
Of kindness linger on

             C
When she no longer needs you.

Verse 2

    C   Em/B
She wakes up,   she makes up,

Am   C/G
She takes her time

   Fmaj7   Bb
And doesn't feel she has to hurry,

         C
She no longer needs you.

Chorus 1

      Dm   A7
And in her eyes you see nothing,

Dm   A7
No sign of love behind the tears cried for no one,

Dm   Gsus G7
A love that should have lasted years.

Copyright © 1966 Sony/ATV Music Publishing LLC
Copyright Renewed
All Rights Administered by Sony/ATV Music Publishing LLC, 8 Music Square West, Nashville, TN 37203
International Copyright Secured   All Rights Reserved

Verse 3

C   Em/B
You want her,   you need her,

Am   C/G
And yet, you don't believe her

Fmaj7   B♭
When she says her love is dead,

     C
You think she needs you.

Solo

|C Em/B |Am C/G |Fmaj7 B♭ |C |

Chorus 2

Repeat Chorus 1

Verse 4

C   Em/B
You stay home,   she goes out,

Am   C/G   Fmaj7
She says that long ago she knew someone,

   B♭
But now she's gone,

   C
She doesn't need him.

Verse 5

C   Em/B
Your day breaks,   your mind aches,

Am   C/G   Fmaj7
There will be times when all the things she said

   B♭
Will fill your head,

C
You won't forget her.

Chorus 3

          Dm   A7
And in her eyes you see nothing,

Dm   A7
No sign of love behind the tears cried for no one,

Dm   Gsus G7
A love that should have lasted years.

For You Blue

Words and Music by
George Harrison

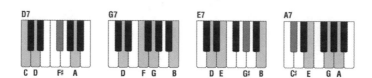

D7   C D   F#   A
G7   D   F G   B
E7   D E   G#   B
A7   C#   E   G A

Intro | D7 | G7 | E7 | A7 | | |

Verse 1

      D7   G7
Be-cause you're sweet and lovely,

      D7
Girl, I love you.

     G7   D7
Be-cause you're sweet and lovely, girl, it's true.

    A7   G7   D7 A7
I love you more than ever, girl, I do.

Verse 2

      D7   G7
I want you in the morning,

      D7
Girl, I love you.

    G7   D7
I want you at the moment I feel blue,

    A7   G7   D7 A7
I'm living every moment, girl, for you.

Copyright © 1970 Harrisongs Ltd.
Copyright Renewed 1998
All Rights Reserved

Solo	|D7 |G7 |D7	|G7		
	(Bop.) (Bop, cat, bop!)
	|D7	|A7 |G7 |D7 |A7	
	(Go Johnny, go!) (Same old twelve-bar blues.)
	|D7 |G7 |D7		
	|G7	|D7		
	(Elmore James got nothing on this baby.)
	|A7 |G7 |D7 |A7	

Verse 3

    D7   G7   D7
I've loved you from the moment I saw you,

    G7   D7
You looked at me, that's all you had to do.

  A7   G7   D7 A7
I feel it now, I hope you feel it too.

Verse 4

    D7   G7
Be-cause you're sweet and lovely,

    D7
Girl, I love you.

  G7   D7
Be-cause you're sweet and lovely, girl, it's true.

  A7   G7   D7
I love you more than ever, girl, I do.

From Me to You

Words and Music by John Lennon
and Paul McCartney

Melody:

Da, da,   da,   da, da, dum, dum,   da.

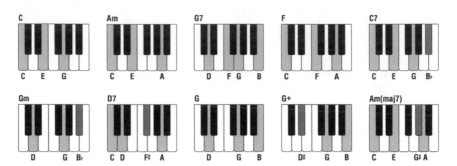

Intro

        C   Am
Da, da, da, da, da, dum, dum, da,

        C   Am
Da, da, da, da, da, dum, dum, da.

Verse 1

       C   Am
If there's anything that you want,

        C   G7
If there's anything I can do,

      F   Am
Just call on me and I'll send it along,

       C   G7   C   Am
With love from me to you.

Verse 2

       C   Am
I've got everything that you want,

       C   G7
Like a heart that's oh so true,

      F   Am
Just call on me and I'll send it along,

       C   G7   C   C7
With love from me to you.

Copyright © 1963 by NORTHERN SONGS LTD., London, England
Copyright Renewed
All rights for the U.S.A., its territories and possessions and Canada assigned to and controlled by
GIL MUSIC CORP., 1650 Broadway, New York, NY 10019
International Copyright Secured   All Rights Reserved

Bridge 1

        Gm   **C**
I got arms that long to hold you,

      F
And keep you by my side,

      D7
I got lips that long to kiss you,

     G   **G+**
And keep you satis-fied.

Verse 3   *Repeat Verse 1*

Solo |C |Am   From me.

        |C |G7   To you.

       F   **Am**
Just call on me and I'll send it along,

     C   **G7**   **C**   **C7**
With love from me to you.

Bridge 2

        Gm   **C**
I got arms that long to hold you,

      F
And keep you by my side,

      D7
I got lips that long to kiss you,

     G   **G+**
And keep you satis-fied.

Verse 4

        C   **Am**
If there's anything that you want,

        C   **G7**
If there's anything I can do,

      F   **Am**
Just call on me and I'll send it along,

     C   **G7**   **C**
With love from me to you.

    Am
To you,

    Am(maj7)
To you,

    C **Am**
To you.

Getting Better

Words and Music by John Lennon
and Paul McCartney

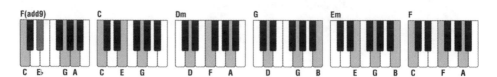

Intro
| F(add9) | |

C   Dm7
It's getting better all the time.

Verse 1
G   C/G
I used to get mad at my school,

G   C/G
The teachers that taught me weren't cool.

G
You're holding me down, turning me 'round,

C/G
Filling me up with your rules.

Chorus 1
C   Dm
I've got to admit, it's getting bet-ter,

Em   F
A little bet-ter all the time.

C   Dm
I have to admit, it's getting bet-ter,

Em   F   G   C/G
It's getting bet-ter since you've been mine.

Copyright © 1967 Sony/ATV Music Publishing LLC
Copyright Renewed
All Rights Administered by Sony/ATV Music Publishing LLC, 8 Music Square West, Nashville, TN 37203
International Copyright Secured   All Rights Reserved

PIANO CHORD SONGBOOK

Verse 2

   G **C/G** **G** **C/G**
Me used to be angry young man,

   G **C/G** **G** **C/G**
Me hiding me head in the sand.

   G   **C/G**
You gave me the word,

  G **C/G**
I finally heard

   G **C/G** **G** **C/G**
I'm doing the best that I can.

Chorus 2

   C   **Dm**
I've got to admit, it's getting bet-ter,

     Em   **F**
A little bet-ter all the time.

  C   **Dm**
I have to admit, it's getting bet-ter,

     Em **F**
It's getting bet-ter since you've been mine.

Getting so much better all the time.

Chorus 3

  C   **Dm**
‖: It's getting better all the time,

  Em   **F**
Bet-ter, better, bet-ter. :‖
|G | |

Verse 3

         G
I used to be cruel to my woman,

I beat her up and kept her apart

From the things that she loved.
G C/G G   **C/G**   **G**   **C/G**
        Man, I was mean, but I'm changing my scene,
      G   **C/G**   **G** **C/G**
And I'm doing the best that I can.

Chorus 4

C   **Dm**
  I admit, it's getting bet-ter,

         Em   **F**
A little bet-ter all the time.
C   **Dm**
Yes, I admit, it's getting bet-ter,
          Em   **F**
It's getting bet-ter since you've been mine.
               C
Getting so much better all the time.

Outro

   C   **Dm**
‖: It's getting better all the time,
    Em   **F**
Bet-ter, better, bet-ter. :‖
        C
Getting so much better all the time.

Golden Slumbers

Words and Music by John Lennon
and Paul McCartney

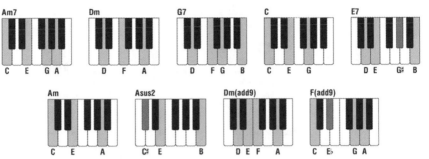

Intro	|**Am7** |

Verse 1	**Am7** **Dm** Once there was a way to get back home-ward,
	G7 **C** Once there was a way to get back home.
	E7 **Am Asus2 Dm(add9)** Sleep, pretty dar-ling, do not cry,
	G7 **C** And I will sing a lulla-by.

Chorus	**C** **F(add9)** **C** Golden slum-bers fill your eyes,
	F(add9) **C** Smiles a-wake you when you rise.
	E7 **Am Asus2 Dm(add9)** Sleep, pretty dar-ling, do not cry,
	G7 **C** And I will sing a lulla-by.

Verse 2	*Repeat Verse 1*

Copyright © 1969 Sony/ATV Music Publishing LLC
Copyright Renewed
All Rights Administered by Sony/ATV Music Publishing LLC, 8 Music Square West, Nashville, TN 37203
International Copyright Secured   All Rights Reserved

Girl

Words and Music by John Lennon
and Paul McCartney

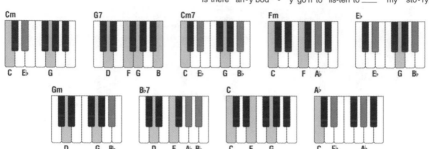

Is there an-y bod - y go'n'to lis-ten to ___ my sto-ry,

Verse 1

           Cm   G7   Cm Cm7
Is there anybody go'n' to listen to my story,

Fm   E♭   G7
All about the girl who came to stay?

           Cm   G7   Cm   Cm7
She's the kind of girl you want so much it makes you sor-ry,

Fm   Cm
Still, you don't regret a single day.

Chorus 1

           E♭ Gm Fm B♭7
Ah, girl.

E♭ Gm Fm B♭7
Girl, girl.

Verse 2

           Cm   G7   Cm   Cm7
When I think of all the times I've tried so hard to leave her,

Fm   E♭ G7
She will turn to me and start to cry.

           Cm   G7   Cm   Cm7
And she promises the earth to me and I be - lieve her,

Fm   Cm
After all this time, I don't know why.

Chorus 2   *Repeat Chorus 1*

Copyright © 1965 Sony/ATV Music Publishing LLC
Copyright Renewed
All Rights Administered by Sony/ATV Music Publishing LLC, 8 Music Square West, Nashville, TN 37203
International Copyright Secured All Rights Reserved

Bridge

Fm
She's the kind of girl

    C
Who puts you down when friends are there,

    Fm C
You feel a fool.

Fm
When you say she's looking good,

  C
She acts as if it's understood,

   Fm   A♭
She's cool, oo, oo, oo.

Chorus 3

E♭ Gm Fm B♭7
Girl.

E♭ Gm Fm B♭7
Girl, girl.

Verse 3

    Cm   G7   Cm   Cm7
Was she told when she was young that pain would lead to pleas-ure?

Fm   E♭   G7
Did she understand it when they said,

    Cm   G7   Cm   Cm7
That a man must break his back to earn his day of leis-ure?

Fm   Cm
Will she still believe it when he's   dead?

Chorus 4   *Repeat Chorus 1*

Solo | Cm G7 | Cm Cm7 | Fm | E♭ G7 |
                    | Cm G7 | Cm Cm7 | Fm | Cm |

Chorus 5

E♭ Gm Fm B♭7
Ah, girl.

E♭ Gm Fm B♭7
Girl, girl.   *Fade out*

Glass Onion

Words and Music by John Lennon
and Paul McCartney

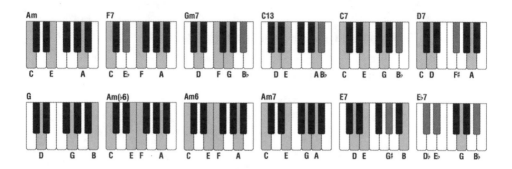

Verse 1

   Am   F7
I told you 'bout Strawberry Fields,

   Am   F7
You know, the place where nothing is real.

   Am   Gm7   C13
Well, here's another place you can go

    Gm7   C7
Where everything flows.

    F7   D7
Look-ing through the bent-backed tulips,

    F7   D7
To see how the other half live.

    F7   G
Look-ing through a glass on-ion.

Copyright © 1968 Sony/ATV Music Publishing LLC
Copyright Renewed
All Rights Administered by Sony/ATV Music Publishing LLC, 8 Music Square West, Nashville, TN 37203
International Copyright Secured   All Rights Reserved

Verse 2

Am   F7
I told you 'bout the walrus and me, man,

Am   F7
You know that we're as close as can be, man.

Am   Gm7   C13
Well, here's another clue for you all…

  Gm7   C7
The walrus was Paul.

 F7   D7
Standing on the cast iron shore, yeah.

F7   D7
Lady Madonna trying to make ends meet, yeah.

F7   G
Looking through a glass on-ion.

Bridge

Am   Am♭6   Am6   Am7
Oh yeah,   oh yeah,   oh yeah!

F7   G
Looking through a glass on-ion.

Verse 3

Am   F7
I told you 'bout the fool on the hill,

Am   F7
I tell you man, he's living there still.

Am   Gm7   C13
Well, here's another place you can be.

Gm7   C7
Listen to me.

F7   D7
Fixing a hole in the ocean,

F7   D7
Trying to make a dovetail join, yeah.

F7   G
Looking through a glass on-ion.

Outro   ‖: F7 | E7 E♭7 | D7 E♭7 E7 | D7 :‖ *Repeat and fade*

Good Day Sunshine

Words and Music by John Lennon
and Paul McCartney

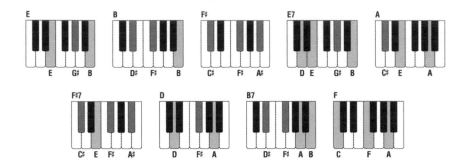

Intro | E | | | |

Chorus 1   Good day sunshine. Good day sunshine.

                  Good day sun-shine.

Verse 1
                          A   F#7   B7
                  I need to laugh,   and when the sun is out,

                  E7   A
                  I've got something I can   laugh about.

                          F#7   B7
                  I feel good   in a spe-cial way,

                  E7   A
                  I'm in love and it's a   sunny day.

Chorus 2   *Repeat Chorus 1*

Copyright © 1966 Sony/ATV Music Publishing LLC
Copyright Renewed
All Rights Administered by Sony/ATV Music Publishing LLC, 8 Music Square West, Nashville, TN 37203
International Copyright Secured   All Rights Reserved

Verse 2

         A   F#7   B7
We take a walk,   the sun is shining down,

E7   A
Burns my feet as they touch the ground.

Solo

| D B7 | E7 | A7 | D |

Chorus 3

Repeat Chorus 1

Verse 3

        A F#7   B7
Then we lie   beneath a shady tree,

E7   A
I love her and she's loving me.

           F#7   B7
She feels good,   she knows she's looking fine.

E7   A
I'm so proud to know that   she is mine.

Chorus 4

Repeat Chorus 1

Chorus 5

B   F#   B   F#
Good day sunshine. Good day sunshine.

E   E7
Good day sun-shine.

    F
‖: Good day sunshine. :‖ *Repeat and fade*

Good Morning Good Morning

Words and Music by John Lennon
and Paul McCartney

Good morn-ing, good morn-ing. Good...

Intro

    A D   **A**   **D**
Good morning, good morning.

    A   **D**
Good morning, good morning.

    A
Good morning, ah!

Verse 1

    A   **Em G**   **A**
Nothing to do to save his life, call his wife in.

    Em   **G**   **A**
Nothing to say but "What a day, how's your boy been?"

D   **E**
Nothing to do, it's up to you.

    A   **Em**   **G**
I've got nothing to say, but it's O.K.

    A   **D**
(Good morning, good morning.

    A
Good morning, ah!)

Copyright © 1967 Sony/ATV Music Publishing LLC
Copyright Renewed
All Rights Administered by Sony/ATV Music Publishing LLC, 8 Music Square West, Nashville, TN 37203
International Copyright Secured   All Rights Reserved

Verse 2

```
A       Em        G              A
Going to work, don't want to go, feeling low down.

             Em      G                     A    D
Heading for home you start to roam, then you're in town.
```

Bridge 1

```
A          D                 A
  Everybody knows there's nothing do-ing,

             D          A
Everything is closed, it's like a ru-in,

             D          A
Everyone you see is half-asleep,

                   D              A
And you're on your own, you're in the street.
```

Verse 3

```
A     Em    G                 A
After a while you start to smile, now you feel cool.

             Em    G           A
Then you de-cide to take a walk by the old school.

D                           E
Nothing has changed, it's all the same,

      A         Em     G
I've got nothing to say, but it's O.K.

      A              D
(Good morning, good morning.

      A
Good morning, ah!)
```

Solo | A Em G | A | Em G| A | D |

                  A   D   A

Bridge 2   People running 'round, it's five o'clock,

                          D   A

Everywhere in town is getting dark,

                          D   A

Everyone you see is full of life,

                          D   A

It's time for tea and meet the wife.

                A   Em   G   A

Verse 4   Somebody needs to know the time, glad that I'm here.

                         Em   G   A

Watching the skirt, you start to flirt, now you're in gear.

                D   E

Go to a show, you hope she goes,

                  A   Em   G

I've got nothing to say, but it's O.K.

                A   D   A

(Good morning, good morning, good!)

                A   D   A   D

‖: (Good morning, good morning, good!) :‖ *Repeat and fade*

A Hard Day's Night

Words and Music by John Lennon
and Paul McCartney

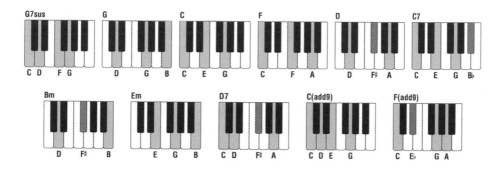

Verse 1

   G7sus   **G**   **C**   **G**
It's been a hard day's night,

             F   **G**
And I've been working like a dog.

          C   **G**
It's been a hard day's night,

           F   **G**
I should be sleeping like a log.

          C
But when I get home to you,

         D
I find the things that you do,

      G **C7** **G**
Will make me feel al - right.

Copyright © 1964 Sony/ATV Music Publishing LLC
Copyright Renewed
All Rights Administered by Sony/ATV Music Publishing LLC, 8 Music Square West, Nashville, TN 37203
International Copyright Secured   All Rights Reserved

Verse 2

<pre>
              G   C G
You know I work all day,

            F   G
To get you money to buy you things.

                     C   G
And it's worth it just to hear you say,

            F   G
You're gonna give me ev'ry-thing.

                 C
So why on earth should I moan,

               D
'Cause when I get you alone,

            G   C7 G
You know I feel O. K.
</pre>

Bridge 1

<pre>
            Bm
When I'm home

Em   Bm
Ev'rything seems to be right.

          G
When I'm home,

Em
Feeling you holding me

C7   D7
Tight, tight, yeah.
</pre>

Verse 3

Repeat Verse 1

| *Solo* | ‖: G C | G | F | G :‖ |

                                C

Verse 4   So why on earth should I moan,

                                    D

          'Cause when I get you alone,

                          G C7 G

          You know I feel O. K.

Bridge 2   *Repeat Bridge 1*

Verse 5   *Repeat Verse 1*

          C7   G C7 G

Outro   You know I feel al - right,

          C7   G C(add9) F(add9) F

          You know I feel al -   right.

          ‖: F(add9) F | F(add9) F :‖ *Repeat and fade*

Good Night

Words and Music by John Lennon
and Paul McCartney

Melody:

Now   it's   time   to   say   good night,

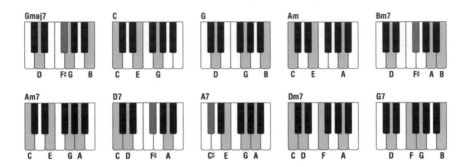

Intro

| Gmaj7 C/G | Gmaj7 C/G | G   Am/G |
| G   Am/G | G   Bm7 | Am7   D7 |

Verse 1

G   Bm7   Am7
Now it's time to say good night,

Bm7 Am7 Am/G D7/F#
Good night, sleep   tight.

G   Bm7   Am7
Now the sun turns out his light,

Bm7 Am7 Am/G D7/F#
Good night, sleep   tight.

Gmaj7   D7/G   Gmaj7   D7/G
Dream sweet dreams for me,

G   C/G   G   C/G
Dream sweet dreams for you.

Copyright © 1968 Sony/ATV Music Publishing LLC
Copyright Renewed
All Rights Administered by Sony/ATV Music Publishing LLC, 8 Music Square West, Nashville, TN 37203
International Copyright Secured   All Rights Reserved

Verse 2

G   Bm7   Am7
Close your eyes and I'll close mine,

Bm7 Am7 Am/G D7/F♯
Good night, sleep   tight.

G   Bm7   Am7
Now the moon be-gins to shine,

Bm7 Am7 Am/G D7/F♯
Good night, sleep   tight.

Gmaj7   D7/G   Gmaj7 D7/G
Dream sweet dreams for me,

G   C/G   G C/G
Dream sweet dreams for you.

Bridge

| G Am7 | A7 Dm7 | G7 C/G | D7/F♯ Am7 D7 |
Mm,   mm,   mm.

Verse 3

G   Bm7   Am7
Close your eyes and I'll close mine,

Bm7 Am7 Am/G D7/F♯
Good night, sleep   tight.

G   Bm7   Am7
Now the sun turns out his light,

Bm7 Am7 Am/G D7/F♯
Good night, sleep   tight.

Gmaj7   D7/G   Gmaj7 D7/G
Dream sweet dreams for me,

G   C/G   G C/G
Dream sweet dreams for you.

Outro

| G Bm7 | Am7 D7 |
            Good night,

G   Bm7
  Good night every-body.

Am7
Everybody everywhere,

D7   G
  Good night.

Got to Get You Into My Life

Words and Music by John Lennon
and Paul McCartney

Melody:

I was a-lone, __ I took a ride, __

G   F   Bm   Bm(maj7)   Bm7

C   Am7   D7   D

Intro

| G | | | | |

Verse 1

G
   I was alone, I took a ride,
                     F/G
I didn't know what I would find there.
G
   Another road where maybe I
                     F/G
Could see another kind of mind there.

Pre-Chorus 1

Bm Bm(maj7) Bm7   Bm/G♯
Ooh,   then I suddenly see you.
Bm Bm(maj7) Bm7   Bm/G♯
Ooh,   did I tell you I need you
C   C/B Am7 D7 G
Ev'ry single day   of my life?

Verse 2

G
   You didn't run, you didn't lie,
                   F/G
You knew I wanted just to hold you.
G
   And had you gone, you knew in time
                   F/G
We'd meet again, for I had told you.

Copyright © 1966 Sony/ATV Music Publishing LLC
Copyright Renewed
All Rights Administered by Sony/ATV Music Publishing LLC, 8 Music Square West, Nashville, TN 37203
International Copyright Secured   All Rights Reserved

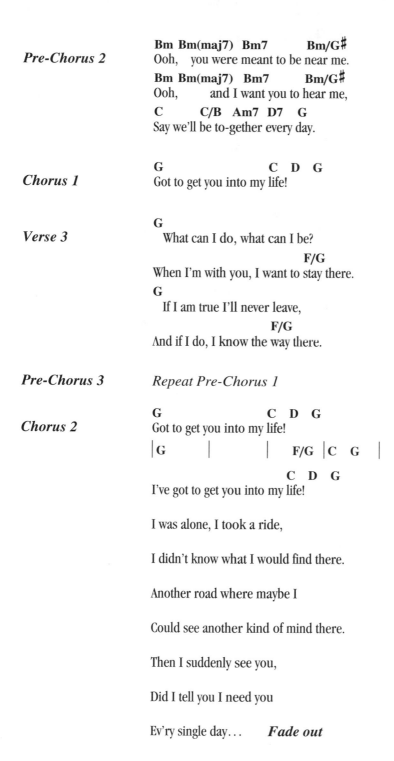

Pre-Chorus 2

Bm Bm(maj7) Bm7   Bm/G♯
Ooh,   you were meant to be near me.

Bm Bm(maj7) Bm7   Bm/G♯
Ooh,   and I want you to hear me,

C   C/B Am7 D7 G
Say we'll be to-gether every day.

Chorus 1

G   C D G
Got to get you into my life!

Verse 3

G
  What can I do, what can I be?
                           F/G
When I'm with you, I want to stay there.
G
  If I am true I'll never leave,
                   F/G
And if I do, I know the way there.

Pre-Chorus 3

Repeat Pre-Chorus 1

Chorus 2

G   C D G
Got to get you into my life!

|G | | F/G |C G |

                   C D G
I've got to get you into my life!

I was alone, I took a ride,

I didn't know what I would find there.

Another road where maybe I

Could see another kind of mind there.

Then I suddenly see you,

Did I tell you I need you

Ev'ry single day...   ***Fade out***

Happiness Is a Warm Gun

Words and Music by John Lennon
and Paul McCartney

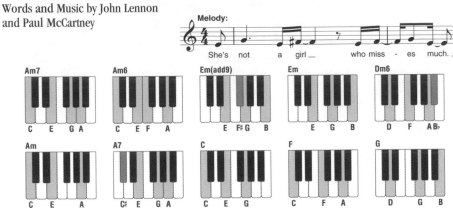

Intro

       Am7 Am6   Em(add9)   Em
She's not a girl who misses much.

   Am7   **Am6 Em(add9) Em**
 Do, do, do, do, do, do,   oh yeah.

Verse 1

   Dm6
 She's well acquainted with the touch

Of the velvet hand,

      Am
Like a lizard on a window pane.

  Dm6
The man in the crowd,

                      Am
With the multicolored mirrors on his hobnail boots.

Dm6
Lying with his eyes,

               Am
While his hands are busy working overtime.

Dm6
 A soap impression of his wife, which he ate,

      Am
And donated to the National Trust.

| A7 | | | C | Am |

Copyright © 1968 Sony/ATV Music Publishing LLC
Copyright Renewed
All Rights Administered by Sony/ATV Music Publishing LLC, 8 Music Square West, Nashville, TN 37203
International Copyright Secured   All Rights Reserved

Verse 2

A7
I need a fix, 'cause I'm going down.

Down to the bits that I left uptown,

C   Am
I need a fix, 'cause I'm going down.

Verse 3

A7   C
‖: Mother Superior, jump the gun,

A7   G
Mother Superior, jump the gun. :‖ *Play 3 times*

Verse 4

C   Am   F   G   C
  Happi-ness is a warm gun,
                          (Bang, bang, shoot, shoot.)

        Am   F   G   C
Happi-ness is a warm gun, mom-ma.
                    (Bang, bang, shoot, shoot.)

        Am   F   G
When I hold you   in my arms,

C   Am   F   G
  And I feel my finger on your trigger,

C Am   F   G
  I know no-body can do me no harm,

C
Because

        Am   F   G   C
Happi-ness is a warm gun, mom-ma.
                          (Bang, bang, shoot, shoot.)

C   Am   F   G   Fm
  Happi-ness is a warm gun, yes it is.
                          (Bang, bang, shoot, shoot.)

                        N.C.
Happiness is a warm gun, yes it is...

        C   Am   F   G
Gun.   Well, don't you know that
            (Happiness. Bang, bang, shoot, shoot.)

C   Am   F   G   C
Happiness   is a warm gun, mom-ma?
            (Happiness...   is a warm gun, yeah!)

Hello, Goodbye

Words and Music by John Lennon
and Paul McCartney

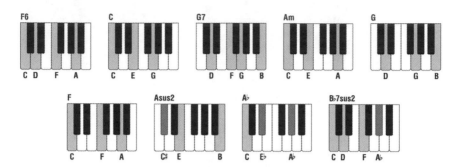

Verse 1

F6   C
You say yes, I say no.

G7   Am   G7
You say stop, but I say go, go, go.

Am G7
  Oh no.

G   G7   F/G
You say good-bye and I say

Chorus 1

      C C/B   Am Asus2/G
Hel-lo,   hello, hel-lo.

           F   Ab
I don't know why you say good-bye, I say

      C C/B   Am Asus2/G
Hel-lo,   hello, hel-lo.

           F   Bb7sus2   C
I don't know why you say good-bye, I say hel-lo.

Copyright © 1967 Sony/ATV Music Publishing LLC
Copyright Renewed
All Rights Administered by Sony/ATV Music Publishing LLC, 8 Music Square West, Nashville, TN 37203
International Copyright Secured   All Rights Reserved

Verse 2

F6   C
I say high, you say low,

G7   Am   G7
You say why and I say I don't know.

Am G7
 Oh no.

G   G7   F/G
You say good-bye and I say hello.

Chorus 2

C   C/B   Am
(Hello, goodbye, hel-lo, goodbye.)
                 Hello, hello.

Asus2/G   F   Ab   C
(Hello, goodbye.)
      I don't know why you say goodbye, I say hello.

C   C/B   Am
(Hello, goodbye, hel-lo, goodbye.)
                 Hello, hello.

Asus2/G   F   Bb7sus2   C
(Hello, goodbye.)
      I don't know why you say goodbye, I say hello.
                (Hello, goodbye.)

Bridge

F6 C   G7
   Why, why, why, why, why, why,

      Am   G7
Do you say goodbye, good-bye?

Am G7
 Oh no.

G   G7   F/G
You say good-bye and I say

Chorus 3	*Repeat Chorus 1*

Verse 3

F6   C
You say yes,   I say no,
                (I say yes, but I may mean no.)

G7   Am   G7
You say stop,   but I say go, go, go.
               (I can stay till it's time to go.)

Am G7
 Oh no

G   G7   F/G
You say good-bye, and I say

Chorus 4	*Repeat Chorus 1*

Chorus 5

C/B   Am Asus2/G
 Hello, hel-lo,

                   F   A♭   A♭/G   F
I don't know why you say good-bye, I say hello,

   C
Hel-lo.

Outro

   C
‖: Hela, heba, helloa. :‖ *Repeat and fade*

Helter Skelter

Words and Music by John Lennon
and Paul McCartney

When I   get   to the bot-tom I   go back to the top of the slide,

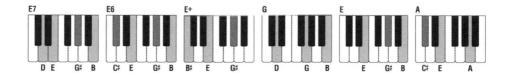

Intro | E7 |

Verse 1

          E7   **E6**
When I get to the bottom I go back to the top of the slide,

                                      E+
Where I stop and turn and I go for a ride,

                                    G
Till I get to the bottom, and I see you a-gain,

          E
Yeah, yeah, yeah!

Verse 2

     E
Do you, don't you want me to love you?

I'm coming down fast, but I'm miles above you.

Tell me, tell me, tell me,

       G
Come on, tell me the answer.

      A   **E**
Well, you may be a lover, but you ain't no danc-er.

Copyright © 1968 Sony/ATV Music Publishing LLC
Copyright Renewed
All Rights Administered by Sony/ATV Music Publishing LLC, 8 Music Square West, Nashville, TN 37203
International Copyright Secured   All Rights Reserved

Chorus 1	A E Helter Skelter, Helter Skelter. A E Helter Skelter, yeah!

Chorus 1

    A   E
Helter Skelter, Helter Skelter.

    A   E
Helter Skelter, yeah!

Verse 3

E
Will you, won't you want me to make you?

I'm coming down fast, but don't let me break you.

G
Tell me, tell me, tell me the answer.

      A   E
You may be a lover, but you ain't no danc-er.

Look out!

Chorus 2

    A   E
Helter Skelter, Helter Skelter.

    A   E
Helter Skelter, yeah!

E
   Look out 'cause here she comes!

Solo

|A |E |A |E |

Verse 4

Repeat Verse 1

Verse 5

E
Well, do you, don't you want me to make you?

I'm coming down fast, but don't let me break you.

G
Tell me, tell me, tell me your answer.

        A   E
Well, you may be a lover, but you ain't no danc-er.

Look out!

Chorus 3

A   E
Helter Skelter, Helter Skelter.

A
Helter Skelter.

E
  Look out! Helter Skelter!

She's coming down fast!

Yes she is, yes she is, coming down fast.

Outro

‖: E7 | :‖   *Repeat and fade*

Hello Little Girl

Words and Music by John Lennon
and Paul McCartney

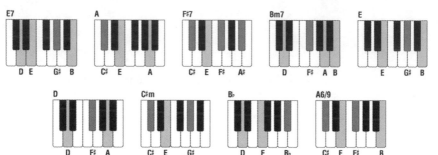

Intro

N.C. **E7**   **A**   **F#7 Bm7**
Hello, little girl,

E7   **A**   **F#7 Bm7**
Hello, little girl,

E7   **A**   **F#7 Bm7 E7**
Hello, little girl.

Verse 1

         A   **E**
When I see you every day

D   **E7 D**   **E**   **A**
I say, mm, mm,   hel-lo, little girl.

                       E
When you're passing on your way

D   **E7 D**   **E**   **A**
I say, mm, mm,   hel-lo, little girl.

Verse 2

         A   **E**
When I see you passing by

D   **E7 D**   **E**   **A**
I cry, mm, mm,   hel-lo, little girl.

                   E
When I try to catch your eye

D   **E7 D**   **E**   **A**
I cry, mm, mm,   hel-lo, little girl.

Copyright © 1963, 1964 Sony/ATV Music Publishing LLC
Copyright Renewed
All Rights Administered by Sony/ATV Music Publishing LLC, 8 Music Square West, Nashville, TN 37203
International Copyright Secured   All Rights Reserved

Bridge 1

A   F♯7   Bm7   E7
I send you flowers, but you don't care,

A   F♯7   Bm7   E7
You never seem to see me standing there.

A   F♯7   Bm7   E7
I often wonder what you're thinking of,

A   F♯7   Bm7   E7
I hope it's me and love, love, love.

Verse 3

        A   E   D
So I hope there'll come a day when you'll say

    E7 D   E   A
Mm, mm, you're my little girl.

Solo

|A   E |D   E |D   E |A |

Bridge 2

A   F♯7   Bm7   E7
It's not the first time that it's happened to me,

A   F♯7   Bm7   E7
It's been a long, lonely time.

A   F♯7   Bm7   E7
And it's so funny, so funny to see

A   F♯7   Bm7 E7
That I'm about to lose my mi-mi-mind.

Verse 4

        A   E   D
So I hope there'll come a day when you'll say

    E7 D   E   A
Mm, mm, you're my little girl.

Outro

    F♯7 Bm7   E   A
Mm, mm, you're my little girl.

    F♯7 Bm7   E   A
Mm, mm, you're my little girl.

    F♯7 Bm7   E   A C♯m Bm7 B♭ A A6/9
Oh yeah, you're my little girl.

Help!

Words and Music by John Lennon
and Paul McCartney

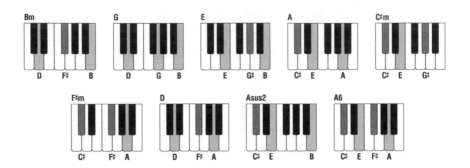

Intro

    Bm
(Help!) I need somebody.

    G
(Help!) Not just anybody.

    E
(Help!) You know I need someone.

    A
(Help!)

Verse 1

  A   **C♯m**
  When I was younger, so much younger than today,

F♯m   **D**   **G A**
  I never needed anybody's help in any way.

  A   **C♯m**
  But now those days are gone and I'm not so self-assured,

F♯m   **D**   **G**   **A**
  Now I find I've changed my mind, and opened up the doors.

Copyright © 1965 Sony/ATV Music Publishing LLC
Copyright Renewed
All Rights Administered by Sony/ATV Music Publishing LLC, 8 Music Square West, Nashville, TN 37203
International Copyright Secured   All Rights Reserved

Chorus 1

Bm
Help me if you can, I'm feeling down,

    G
And I do appreciate you being 'round.

E
Help me get my feet back on the ground.

        A   **A Asus2 A Asus2 A**
Won't you please, please help me?

Verse 2

A   **C♯m**
And now my life has changed in oh, so many ways.

F♯m   **D**   **G**   **A**
My independence seems to vanish in the haze.

A   **C♯m**
But ev'ry now and then I feel so insecure.

F♯m   **D**   **G**   **A**
I know that I just need you like I've never done be-fore.

Chorus 2   *Repeat Chorus 1*

Verse 3   *Repeat Verse 1*

Chorus 3

Bm
Help me if you can, I'm feeling down,

    G
And I do appreciate you being 'round.

E
Help me get my feet back on the ground.

        A   **F♯m**
Won't you please, please help me?

        A **A6**
Help me, help me, ooh, mm.

Her Majesty

Words and Music by John Lennon
and Paul McCartney

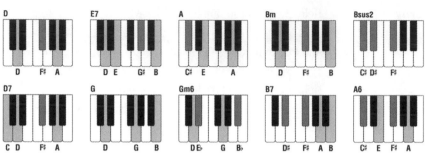

Intro |D |

Verse

    D   D/C#   D/B   D/A
Her Majesty's a pretty nice girl,

         E7   A   D
But she doesn't have a lot to say.

    D/C#   D/B   D/A
Her Majesty's a pretty nice girl,

         E7   A
But she changes from day to day.

Bm   Bsus2
  I wanna tell her that I love her a lot,

  D7   G
But I gotta get a belly full of wine.

Gm6   D   B7
  Her Majesty's a pretty nice girl,

      E7   A6   D
Some day I'm gonna make her mine,

      B7
Oh yeah,

      E7   A6   D
Some day I'm gonna make her mine.

Copyright © 1969 Sony/ATV Music Publishing LLC
Copyright Renewed
All Rights Administered by Sony/ATV Music Publishing LLC, 8 Music Square West, Nashville, TN 37203
International Copyright Secured   All Rights Reserved

Hey Jude

Words and Music by John Lennon
and Paul McCartney

Hey   Jude, _____ don't make it   bad.

Verse 1

    F   **C7**
Hey Jude, don't make it bad.

                   F
Take a sad song and make it better.

  B♭   **F**
Re-member to let her into your heart,

         C7   **F**
Then you can start to make it bet-ter.

Verse 2

    F   **C7**
Hey Jude, don't be afraid.

                   F
You were made to go out and get her.

  B♭   **F**
The minute you let her under your skin,

         C7   **F**   **F7**
Then you be-gin to make it bet-ter.

Copyright © 1968 Sony/ATV Music Publishing LLC
Copyright Renewed
All Rights Administered by Sony/ATV Music Publishing LLC, 8 Music Square West, Nashville, TN 37203
International Copyright Secured   All Rights Reserved

Bridge 1

                               B♭
And anytime you feel the pain,

    B♭/A   **B♭/G**
Hey Jude, re-frain.

       B♭/F   **C7**   **F**   **F7**
Don't car-ry the world upon your shoulders.

                        B♭
For well you know that it's a fool

    B♭/A   **B♭/G**
Who plays it cool

      B♭/F   **C7**   **F**
By mak-ing his world a little colder.

      F7   **C7**
Na, na, na, na, na, na, na, na, na.

Verse 3

       F   **C7**
Hey Jude, don't let me down.

                         F
You have found her, now go and get her.

    B♭   **F**
Re-member to let her into your heart,

         C7   **F**   **F7**
Then you can start to make it bet-ter.

Bridge 2

             B♭
So let it out and let it in,

    B♭/A   **B♭/G**
Hey Jude, be-gin,

      B♭/F   **C7**   **F**   **F7**
You're wait-ing for some-one to per-form with.

               B♭
And don't you know that it's just you,

   B♭/A   **B♭/G**
Hey Jude, you'll do.

    B♭/F   **C7**   **F**
The movement you need is on your shoulder.

      F7   **C7**
Na, na, na, na, na, na, na, na, na. Yeah.

Verse 4

    F   **C7**
Hey Jude, don't make it bad.

                     F
Take a sad song and make it better.

  B♭   **F**
Re-member to let her under your skin,

       C7   **F**
Then you be-gin to make it bet-ter,

Better, better, better, better, better, oh.

Outro

  F   **E♭**
‖: Na,   na, na,   na, na, na, na,

B♭   **F**
Na, na, na, na.   Hey Jude. :‖ *Repeat and fade*

Here Comes the Sun

Words and Music by
George Harrison

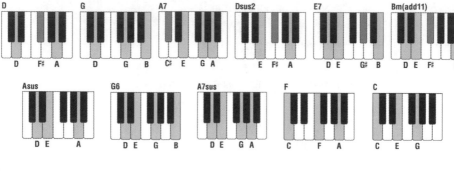

Intro

‖: D | | G | A7 :‖

Chorus 1

D   Dsus2 D
Here comes the sun,

G   E7
Here comes the sun,

        D   Dsus2 D
And I say it's all   right.

| Bm(add11) Asus | G6 Asus A7 |

Verse 1

D   Dsus2 D   G   A7   A7sus
Little dar - ling, it's been a long, cold, lonely win - ter.

D   Dsus2 D   G   A7 A7sus
Little dar - ling, it feels like years since it's been here.

Chorus 2

D   Dsus2 D
Here comes the sun,

G   E7
Here comes the sun,

        D   Dsus2 D
And I say it's all   right.

| Bm(add11) Asus | G6 Asus A7 | D | A7 |

Copyright © 1969 Harrisongs Ltd.
Copyright Renewed 1998
All Rights Reserved

	D Dsus2 D G A7 A7sus
Verse 2	Little dar - ling, the smile's re-turning to their faces,

D   Dsus2 D   G   A7 A7sus
Little dar - ling, it seems like years since it's been here.

Chorus 3   *Repeat Chorus 2*

Bridge
```
|F     |C     |G/B  |G     |D     |A7    |

‖:F     |C     |G/B  |G     |D     |A7   :‖  Play 5 times
 Sun,     sun,    sun,    here it comes.

|A7    |A7sus |A7   |A7sus  A     |
```

D   Dsus2 D   G   A7   A7sus
Verse 3   Little dar - ling, I feel that ice is slowly melt - ing.

D   Dsus2 D   G   A7 A7sus
Little dar - ling, it seems like years since it's been clear.

Chorus 4   *Repeat Chorus 1*

Chorus 5
D   Dsus2 D
Here comes the sun,

G   E7
Here comes the sun,

D
It's alright.

```
|Bm(add11)  Asus    |G6  Asus   A7|
```

D
It's all right.

```
|Bm(add11)  Asus    |G6  Asus   A7|

|F    C   |G/B G   |D/A
```

Here, There and Everywhere

Words and Music by John Lennon
and Paul McCartney

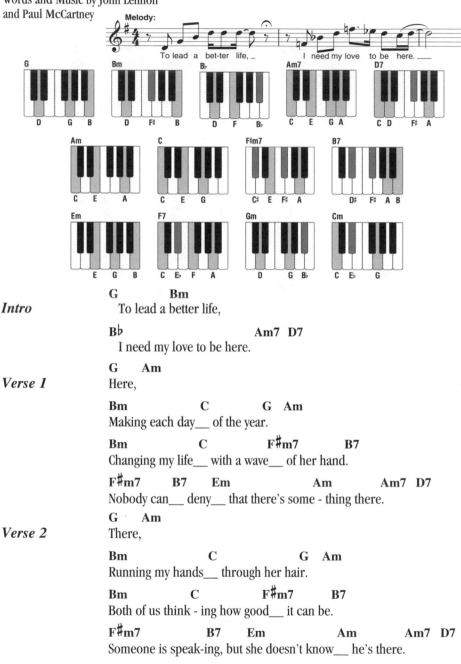

Intro

	G	Bm

To lead a better life,

Bb   Am7   D7

I need my love to be here.

Verse 1

G   Am

Here,

Bm   C   G   Am

Making each day___ of the year.

Bm   C   F#m7   B7

Changing my life___ with a wave___ of her hand.

F#m7   B7   Em   Am   Am7   D7

Nobody can___ deny___ that there's some - thing there.

Verse 2

G   Am

There,

Bm   C   G   Am

Running my hands___ through her hair.

Bm   C   F#m7   B7

Both of us think - ing how good___ it can be.

F#m7   B7   Em   Am   Am7   D7

Someone is speak-ing, but she doesn't know___ he's there.

Copyright © 1966 Sony/ATV Music Publishing LLC
Copyright Renewed
All Rights Administered by Sony/ATV Music Publishing LLC, 8 Music Square West, Nashville, TN 37203
International Copyright Secured   All Rights Reserved

Bridge 1

F7   Bb   Gm
I want her ev'rywhere,

      Cm   D7   Gm
And if she's beside me, I know I need never care.

Cm   D7
But to love her is to need her

Verse 3

G   Am
Ev'rywhere.

Bm   C   G Am
Knowing that love__ is to share.

Bm   C   F#m7   B7
Each one believ - ing that love__ never dies,

F#m7   B7   Em   Am   Am7 D7
Watching their eyes__ and hoping I'm al - ways there.

Bridge 2

F7   Bb   Gm
I want her ev'rywhere,

      Cm   D7   Gm
And if she's beside me, I know I need never care.

Cm   D7
But to love her is to need her

Verse 4

G   Am
Ev'rywhere.

Bm   C   G Am
Knowing that love__ is to share.

Bm   C   F#m7   B7
Each one believ - ing that love__ never dies.

F#m7   B7   Em   Am   Am7 D7
Watching her eyes__ and hoping I'm al - ways there.

      G Am
I will be there

    Bm   C
And ev'rywhere.

G Am   Bm   C   G
Here, there and ev'rywhere.

Hey Bulldog

Words and Music by John Lennon
and Paul McCartney

Melody:

Sheep dog ___ stand-ing in the rain,

Intro	‖: **B7** | :‖ *Play 3 times*

Verse 1

    B7   **F♯m7**
    Sheep dog standing in the rain,

    B7   **F♯m7**
    Bullfrog, doing it again.

    A   **F♯m7**   **E**   **E7**
    Some kind of happiness is measured out in miles.

    A   **F♯m7**   **B7**
    What makes you think you're something special when you smile?

Verse 2

    B7   **F♯m7**
    Child-like, no one understands,

    B7   **F♯m7**
    Jack-knife in your sweaty hands.

    A   **F♯m7**   **E**   **E7**
    Some kind of innocence is measured out in years,

    A   **F♯m7**   **B7**
    You don't know what it's like to listen to your fears.

Copyright © 1968, 1969 Sony/ATV Music Publishing LLC
Copyright Renewed
All Rights Administered by Sony/ATV Music Publishing LLC, 8 Music Square West, Nashville, TN 37203
International Copyright Secured   All Rights Reserved

Chorus 1

      Bm   **Bm(add♯5)** **Bm6**
You can talk to   me.

      Bm7   **Em** **Em(add♯5)**
You can talk to me.

      Em6   **Em7**
You can talk to me.

            Bm   **Em** **B7**
If you're lonely, you can talk to me.

Solo

| **B7** | **F♯m7** | **B7** | **F♯m7** | |
| **A** **F♯m7** | **E** **E7** | **A** **F♯m7** | **B7** | |

Verse 3

B7   **F♯m7**
 Big man, walking in the park.

B7   **F♯m7**
 Wigwam, frightened of the dark.

A   **F♯m7**   **E**   **E7**
 Some kind of solitude is measured out in you.

A   **F♯m7**   **B7**
 You think you know me, but you haven't got a clue.

Chorus 2   *Repeat Chorus 1*

Outro   ‖: **F♯m7**   **B7**   :‖ *Repeat and fade*
              Hey, bull-dog.

Hold Me Tight

Words and Music by John Lennon
and Paul McCartney

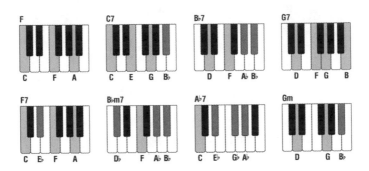

Intro

　　F　　C7
　It feels so right now.

Verse 1

F　　　　Bb7
Hold me tight,

G7　　　　　　　C7
　Tell me I'm the only one,

　　F　　Bb7
And then I might

G7　　　　　C7
　Never be the lonely one.

　　F　　　F7　　Bb7　　Bbm7
So hold me tight, to-night, to-night.

　　F　Bbm7
It's you,

　　　　F　C7
You, you, you.

Copyright © 1963 Sony/ATV Music Publishing LLC
Copyright Renewed
All Rights Administered by Sony/ATV Music Publishing LLC, 8 Music Square West, Nashville, TN 37203
International Copyright Secured   All Rights Reserved

Verse 2	F B♭7
	Hold me tight,
	
	G7 C7
	  Let me go on loving you.
	
	    F B♭7
	To-night, to-night,
	
	G7 C7
	  Making love to only you.
	
	    F F7 B♭7 B♭m7
	So hold me tight, to-night, to-night.
	
	    F B♭m7
	It's you,
	
	         F A♭7
	You, you, you.

Bridge 1	A♭7 F7 A♭7 F7
	  Don't know what it means to hold you tight,
	
	B♭7 Gm G7
	  Being here a-lone tonight with you.
	
	  C7
	It feels so right now.

Verse 3	*Repeat Verse 1*
Bridge 2	*Repeat Bridge 1*

Verse 4	F B♭7
	Hold me tight,
	
	G7 C7
	  Let me go on loving you.
	
	    F B♭7
	To-night, to-night,
	
	G7 C7
	  Making love to only you.
	
	    F F7 B♭7 B♭m7
	So hold me tight, to-night, to-night.
	
	    F B♭m7
	It's you,
	
	         F A♭7 F
	You, you, you.
	
	A♭7 F
	You.

Honey Pie

Words and Music by John Lennon
and Paul McCartney

Melody:

She was a work-ing girl, __

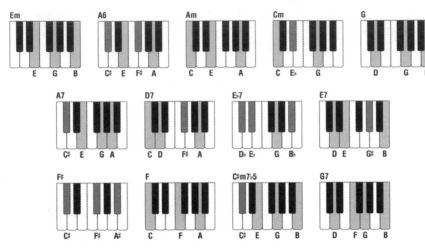

Intro

    Em   **A6**   **Am/D**
    She was a working girl,

Cm   **G**
North of England way.

Em   **A6**   **Am/D Cm**   **G**
Now she's hit the big time   in the U.S.A.

A7
And if she could only hear me,

D7
This is what I'd say:

Verse 1

G   **E♭7**
Honey Pie, you are making me crazy.

E7   **A7**
  I'm in love, but I'm lazy.

D7   **G**   **E♭7**   **D7**
  So won't you please come home?

Copyright © 1968 Sony/ATV Music Publishing LLC
Copyright Renewed
All Rights Administered by Sony/ATV Music Publishing LLC, 8 Music Square West, Nashville, TN 37203
International Copyright Secured   All Rights Reserved

Verse 2

```
          G                         Eb7
Oh, Honey Pie, my position is tragic.

E7                      A7
  Come and show me the magic

D7                    G   F♯   F
  Of your Hollywood song.
```

Bridge 1

```
Em                 C♯m7b5    G
You became a leg-end of the sil-ver screen,

G7            C
  And now the thought of meeting you

E7                      Am    D7
Makes me weak in the knee.
```

Verse 3

```
          G                         Eb7
Oh, Honey Pie, you are driving me frantic,

E7                      A7
  Sail across the At-lantic

D7                    G
  To be where you be-long.

          Eb7        D7      G
Honey Pie, come back to me.
```

Solo

```
|G    |       |Eb7  |E7   |A7   |D7   |
G            Eb7   D7
  (I like it like that.)
```

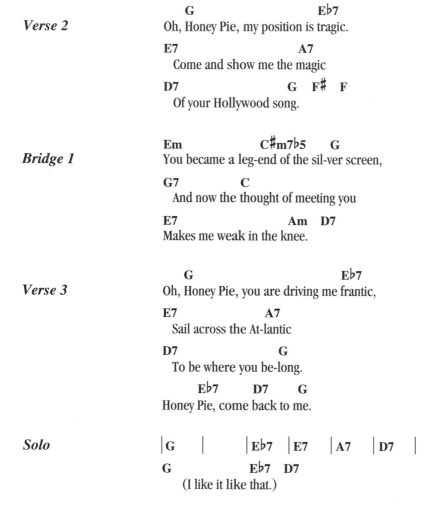

Verse 4

G   Eb7
   …I like this kind of, hot kind of music,

E7
Hot kind of music.

A7
Play it to me,

D7   G   F♯   F
Play it to me, Hollywood blues.

Bridge 2

Em   C♯m7b5   G   G7
Will the wind that blew her boat a-cross the sea

C   E7   Am   D7
  Kindly send her sailing back to me?

Verse 5

      G   Eb7
Now, Honey Pie, you are making me crazy.

E7   A7
  I'm in love, but I'm lazy.

D7   G
  So won't you please come home?

          Eb7   D7   G
(Come, come back to me, Honey Pie.)

| G | Eb7 | E7 | A7 | |

D7   G
(Honey Pie, Honey Pie.)

| Eb7 D7 | G

I Me Mine

Words and Music by
George Harrison

Melody: All _____ through the day, _____

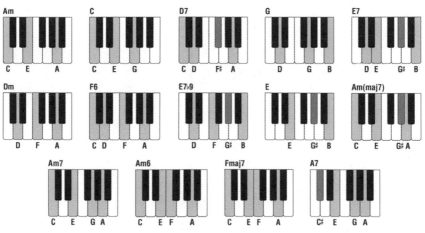

Intro |Am   C |D7 |G   E7 |

Verse 1

Am   C   D7
All _____ through the day,

        G   E7   Am
I me mine, I me mine, I me mine.

            C   D7
All _____ through the night,

        G   E7   Am
I me mine, I me mine, I me mine.

        Dm
Never frightened of leaving it;

F6
Everyone's weaving it.

E7♭9   E
Coming on strong all the time.

Am   Am(maj7)   Am7   Am6
All _____ through the day,

        Fmaj7
I me mine.

Copyright © 1970, 1981 Harrisongs Ltd.
Copyright Renewed 1998
All Rights Reserved

Chorus 1

A7
I me, me mine.

I me, me mine.
D7
  I me, me mine.
A7   **E7**
  I me, me mine.

Verse 2

Am   **C**   **D7**
All _____ I can hear,

    G   **E7**   **Am**
I me mine, I me mine, I me mine.

   C   **D7**
E-ven those tears,

    G   **E7**   **Am**
I me mine, I me mine, I me mine.

      Dm
No one's frightened of playing it;

F6
Everyone's saying it.

E7♭9   **E**
Flowing more freely than wine.

Am **Am(maj7)**   **Am7** **Am6**
All _____ through the day,

    Fmaj7
I me mine.

Chorus 2   *Repeat Chorus 1*

Verse 3

      Am   **C**   **D7**
All _____ I can hear,

      G   **E7**   **Am**
I me mine, I me mine, I me mine.

  C   **D7**
E-ven those tears,

      G   **E7**   **Am**
I me mine, I me mine, I me mine.

        Dm
No one's frightened of playing it;

F6
Everyone's saying it.

E7♭9   **E**
Flowing more freely than wine.

Am **Am(maj7)**   **Am7** **Am6**
All _____ through your life,

      Fmaj7
I me mine.

I Am the Walrus

Words and Music by John Lennon
and Paul McCartney

Melody:

I am he as you are he as...

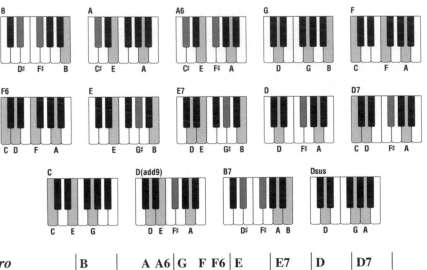

B	A	A6	G	F
D♯ F♯ B	C♯ E A	C♯ E F♯ A	D G B	C F A

F6	E	E7	D	D7
C D F A	E G♯ B	D E G♯ B	D F♯ A	C D F♯ A

C	D(add9)	B7	Dsus
C E G	D E F♯ A	D♯ F♯ A B	D G A

Intro | B | A A6 | G F F6 | E | E7 | D | D7 |

Verse 1
      A   A/G
I am he as you are he

        C   D   A   A/G
As you are me and we are all to-gether.

    C
See how they run like pigs from a gun,

        D   A
See how they fly, I'm crying.

Verse 2
    A   A/G   D(add9)/F♯
Sitting on a corn-flake,

    F   G   A   A/G
Waiting for the van to come.

    F
Corporation T-shirt stupid bloody Tuesday,

    B7
Man, you been a naughty boy, you let your face grow long.

Copyright © 1967 Sony/ATV Music Publishing LLC
Copyright Renewed
All Rights Administered by Sony/ATV Music Publishing LLC, 8 Music Square West, Nashville, TN 37203
International Copyright Secured   All Rights Reserved

Chorus 1

        C   **D**
I am the eggman, they are the eggmen,

        E
I am the walrus,

Goo goo g'joob.

Verse 3

A   **A/G**   **C**   **D**   **A**   **A/G**
Mr. City p'licemen sitting pretty little p'licemen in a row.

C
See how they fly like Lucy in the sky,

       D   **A**
See how they run, I'm crying.

      Dsus
I'm cry - ing,

      A
I'm crying,

      E   **D**   **D7**
I'm cry - ing.

Verse 4

A   **A/G**   **D(add9)/F♯**
Yellow matter custard,

F   **G**   **A**   **A/G**
Dripping from a dead dog's eye.

F
Crabalocker fishwife, pornographic priestess,

B7
Boy, you been a naughty girl, you let your knickers down.

Chorus 2
                        C   D
          I am the eggman, they are the eggmen,

                        E
          I am the walrus,

          Goo goo g'joob.
          | B   A | G   F | E |

                   B   A   G   F   E
Bridge
          Sitting in an English garden, waiting for the sun.
          F   B7
             If the sun don't come, you get a tan

          From standing in the English rain.

                        C   D
Chorus 3
          I am the eggman, they are the eggmen,

                        E
          I am the walrus,

          Goo goo g'joob.

          D
          Goo goo goo g'joob.

                   A   A/G
Verse 5
          Expert texpert choking smokers,

          C   D   A
          Don't you think the joker laughs at you?

                   A/G
          (Ha, ha, ha! Hee, hee, hee! Ha, ha, ha!)

          C
          See how they smile like pigs in the sty,

                D   A
          See how they snied, I'm crying.

Verse 6

A   A/G   Dadd9/F#
Semolina pilchard,

F   G   A   A/G
Climbing up the Eiffel Tower.

F
Elementary penguin singing Hare Krishna,

   B7
Man, you should have seen them

Kicking Edgar Allen Poe.

Chorus 4

        C   D
I am the eggman, they are the eggmen,

        E
I am the walrus,

Goo goo g'joob.

D
Goo goo goo g'joob.

C
Goo goo g'joob.

            B7
Goo goo goo g'joob, goo.

  Chooga, chooga, chooga.

Joob-a, joob-a, joob-a.

‖: A | G | F | E |
  | D | C | B7   :‖ *Repeat and fade*

I Call Your Name

Words and Music by John Lennon
and Paul McCartney

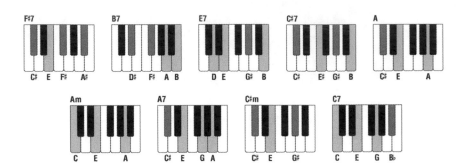

Intro | F#7 | B7 | E7 | B7 |

Verse 1

      E7
I call your name,

         C#7
But you're not there.

      F#7
Was I to blame

        B7
For being un-fair?

      E7
Oh, I can't sleep at night

         C#7
Since you've been gone.

    F#7
I never weep at night,

A Am   **E7**
I can't go on.

Copyright © 1963 Sony/ATV Music Publishing LLC
Copyright Renewed
All Rights Administered by Sony/ATV Music Publishing LLC, 8 Music Square West, Nashville, TN 37203
International Copyright Secured   All Rights Reserved

Bridge 1

                  A7
Don't you know I can't take it?

                   C#m
I don't know who can.

           F#7
I'm not goin' to make it,

                C7   B7
I'm not that kind of man.

Verse 2

         E7
Oh, I can't sleep at night,

       C#7
But just the same

      F#7
I never weep at night,

A Am   E7
  I call your name.

Solo

| E7 | | | C#7 | | |
| F#7 | | A Am | E7 | | |

Bridge 2

Repeat Bridge 1

Verse 3

         E7
Oh, I can't sleep at night,

       C#7
But just the same,

      F#7
I never weep at night.

A Am   E7
  I call your name.

A7   E7
‖: I call your name.

A7   E7
  I call your name. :‖   ***Repeat and fade***

I Don't Want to Spoil the Party

Words and Music by John Lennon
and Paul McCartney

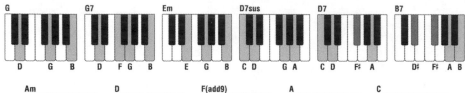

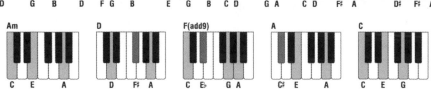

Intro

| G | | G7 Em | D7sus | | |
| D7 | | G | | |

Verse 1

           G
I don't want to spoil the party, so I'll go.

                         D7
I would hate my disappointment to show.

      Em   **B7**   **Am**   **D**
There's nothing for me here, so I will disap-pear.

      G   **F(add9)**   **G**
If she turns up while I'm gone, please let me know.

Verse 2

         G
I've had a drink or two and I don't care.

                       D7
There's no fun in what I do if she's not there.

    Em   **B7**   **Am**   **D**
I wonder what went wrong, I've waited far too long.

  G   **F(add9)**   **G**
I think I'll take a walk and look for her.

Copyright © 1964 Sony/ATV Music Publishing LLC
Copyright Renewed
All Rights Administered by Sony/ATV Music Publishing LLC, 8 Music Square West, Nashville, TN 37203
International Copyright Secured   All Rights Reserved

	G
Bridge 1	Though to-night she's made me sad,

Em A   C   D7
I   still love her.

   G
If I find her I'll be glad,

Em A   C   D7
I   still love her.

Verse 3   *Repeat Verse 1*

Solo

G							
D7		Em	B7	Am	D	
G	F(add9)	G					

Bridge 2   *Repeat Bridge 1*

             G
Verse 4   So, I've had a drink or two and I don't care.

                         D7
There's no fun in what I do if she's not there.

  Em   B7   Am   D
I wonder what went wrong, I've waited far too long.

 G   F(add9)   G
I think I'll take a walk and look for her.

Outro

G	G7 Em	D7sus		
D7		G		

I Feel Fine

Words and Music by John Lennon
and Paul McCartney

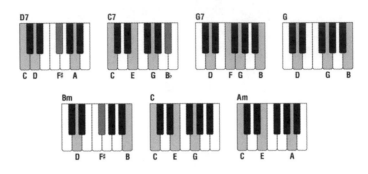

Intro

| D7 | | C7 | | |
| G7 | | | | |

Verse 1

G7
Baby's good to me, you know,

She's happy as can be, you know

D7
She said so.

         C7   G7
I'm in love with her and I feel fine.

Verse 2

G7
Baby says she's mine, you know,

She tells me all the time, you know

D7
She said so.

         C7   G7
I'm in love with her and I feel fine.

Copyright © 1964 Sony/ATV Music Publishing LLC
Copyright Renewed
All Rights Administered by Sony/ATV Music Publishing LLC, 8 Music Square West, Nashville, TN 37203
International Copyright Secured   All Rights Reserved

Bridge 1

G   Bm
I'm so glad
        C   D7
That she's my little girl.
G   Bm
She's so glad,
          Am   D7
She's telling all the world

Verse 3

                G7
That her baby buys her things, you know,

He buys her diamond rings, you know
    D7
She said so.
              C7   G7
She's in love with me and I feel fine.

Solo

G7				D7		
			C7		
G7				

Verse 4

Repeat Verse 2

Bridge 2

Repeat Bridge 1

Verse 5

                G7
That her baby buys her things, you know,

He buys her diamond rings, you know
    D7
She said so.
             C7   G7
She's in love with me and I feel fine.
D7   C7   G7
She's in love with me and I feel fine.

Outro

‖: G7 | | | :‖ *Repeat and fade*

I Need You

Words and Music by
George Harrison

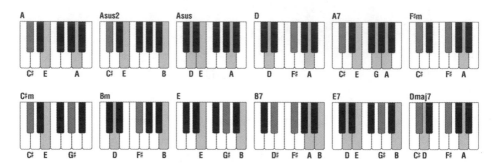

Intro |A   Asus2 |Asus A |

Verse 1

  A   D   A Asus2 Asus A
You don't real-ize how much I need you.

                 D   A A7 Asus A
Love you all the time and never leave you.

    F#m   C#m F#m   Bm
Please come on back to me, I'm lonely as can be.

  A Asus2 Asus A
I need you.

Verse 2

  A   D   A Asus2 Asus A
Said you had a thing or two to tell me.

                 D   A A7 Asus A
How was I to know you would up-set me?

  F#m   C#m F#m   Bm
I didn't real-ize as I looked in your eyes,

  A Asus2 Asus A
You told me.

Copyright © 1965 Sony/ATV Music Publishing LLC
Copyright Renewed
All Rights Administered by Sony/ATV Music Publishing LLC, 8 Music Square West, Nashville, TN 37203
International Copyright Secured   All Rights Reserved

Bridge 1

                  D
Oh yes, you told me

    E   **A**
You don't want my lovin' any-more.

                D   **E**
That's when it hurt me, and feeling like this

B7   **E7**
I just can't go on any-more.

A   **D**   **A**   **Asus2** **Asus** **A**

Verse 3
Please remember how I feel a-bout you.

                D   **A** **A7** **Asus** **A**
I could never really live with-out you.

  F♯m   **C♯m**
So, come on back and see

    F♯m   **Bm**
Just what you mean to me.

  A   **Asus2** **Asus** **A**
I need you.

                D

Bridge 2
But when you told me

    E   **A**
You don't want my lovin' any-more,

               D   **E**
That's when it hurt me, and feeling like this

B7   **E7**
I just can't go on any-more.

A   **D**   **A** **Asus2** **Asus** **A**

Verse 4
Please remember how I feel a-bout you.

                D   **A** **A7** **Asus** **A**
I could never really live with-out you.

    F♯m   **C♯m**
So, come on back and see

    F♯m   **Bm**
Just what you mean to me.

A   **Asus2** **Asus** **A**
I need you.

F♯m   **Dmaj7**
I need you, I need you.

|**A**   **Asus2**|**Asus** **A**

I Saw Her Standing There

Words and Music by John Lennon
and Paul McCartney

Melody:

Well, she was just ___ sev-en - teen, ___

E7   A7   B7   C   E9

D E   G# B   C# E   G A   D#   F# A B   C   E   G   D   F# G# B

Intro | E7 | | | |

Verse 1

          E7
Well, she was just seventeen,

   A7   **E7**
You know what I mean.

                              B7
And the way she looked was way beyond com-pare.

   E7   **A7**
So how could I dance with an-other,

C   **E7**   **B7**   **E7**
Oo, when I saw her standing there.

Verse 2

          E7
Well, she looked at me,

   A7   **E7**
And I, I could see

                              B7
That before too long, I'd fall in love with her.

E7   **A7**
She wouldn't dance with an-other,

C   **E7**   **B7**   **E7**
Oo, when I saw her standing there.

Copyright © 1963 by NORTHERN SONGS LTD., London, England
Copyright Renewed
All Rights for the U.S.A., its territories and possessions and Canada assigned to and controlled by
GIL MUSIC CORP., 1650 Broadway, New York, NY 10019
International Copyright Secured   All Rights Reserved

Bridge 1

          A7
Well, my heart went boom

When I crossed that room,

            B7   **A7**
And I held her hand in mine.

Verse 3

          E7
Well, we danced through the night,

        A7   **E7**
And we held each other tight.

                       B7
And before too long I fell in love with her.

      E7   **A7**
Now I'll never dance with an-other,

      C   **E7**   **B7**   **E7**
Oo, when I saw her standing there.

Solo

E7						
B7		E7		A7		
E7	B7	E7				

Bridge 2

Repeat Bridge 1

Verse 4

          E7
Oh, we danced through the night,

        A7   **E7**
And we held each other tight,

                       B7
And before too long I fell in love with her.

      E7   **A7**
Now I'll never dance with an-other,

      C   **E7**   **B7**   **E7**
Oo, since I saw her standing there.

               B7   **E7**
Oo, since I saw her standing there.

               B7   **A7**   **E7** **E9**
Yeah, well, since I saw her standing there.

I Should Have Known Better

Words and Music by John Lennon
and Paul McCartney

Melody:

I _____ should-'ve known __

Intro

| G D | G D | G D | G D |

Verse 1

G D G D   G   D   G D
I _____ should've known better with a girl like you,

     G   D   Em
That I would love every-thing that you do,

   C   D   G D G
And I do, hey, hey, hey, and I do.

Verse 2

D   G D G D   G   D   G D
Woh, woh, I _____ never real-ized what a kiss could be.

     G   D   Em
This could only happen to me.

     C   B7
Can't you see, can't you see?

Bridge 1

Em   C   G   B7
   That when I tell you that I love you, oh,

Em   G   G7
   You're gonna say you love me too, ___ oh,

C   D   G   Em
   And when I ask you to be mine

C   D   G D G
   You're gonna say you love me too.

Copyright © 1964 Sony/ATV Music Publishing LLC
Copyright Renewed
All Rights Administered by Sony/ATV Music Publishing LLC, 8 Music Square West, Nashville, TN 37203
International Copyright Secured   All Rights Reserved

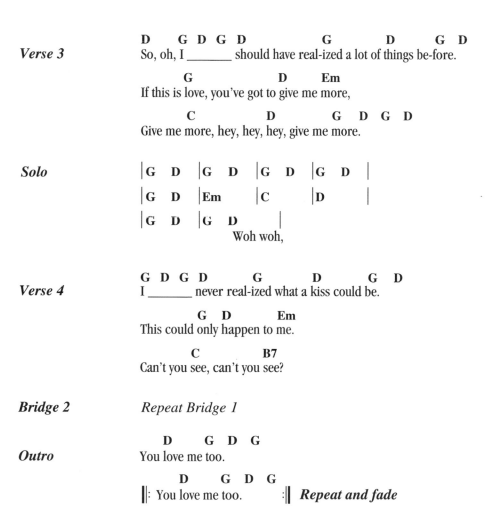

Verse 3

D   G D G D   G   D   G D

So, oh, I _____ should have real-ized a lot of things be-fore.

                G   D   Em

If this is love, you've got to give me more,

          C   D   G D G D

Give me more, hey, hey, hey, give me more.

Solo

G	D	G	D	G	D	G	D	
G	D	Em		C		D		
G	D	G	D		

                   Woh woh,

Verse 4

G D G D   G   D   G D

I _____ never real-ized what a kiss could be.

           G D   Em

This could only happen to me.

         C   B7

Can't you see, can't you see?

Bridge 2

Repeat Bridge 1

Outro

       D   G   D   G

You love me too.

       D   G   D G

‖: You love me too.   :‖ *Repeat and fade*

I Wanna Be Your Man

Words and Music by John Lennon
and Paul McCartney

Melody:

I wan-na be your lov-er, ba - by,

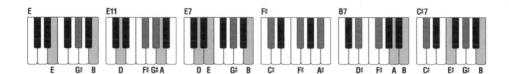

E   E11   E7   F♯   B7   C♯7

Verse 1

   E   E11   E   E11
I wanna be your lover, baby,

   E   E11   E   E11
I wanna be your man.

   E   E11   E   E11
I wanna be your lover, baby,

   E   E11   E7
I wanna be your man.

Verse 2

   E   E11   E   E11
Love you like no other, baby,

   E   E11   E   E11
Like no other can.

   E   E11   E   E11
Love you like no other, baby,

   E   E11   E7
Like no other can.

Copyright © 1964 NORTHERN SONGS LIMITED
Copyright Renewed
All rights for the United States of America, its territories and possessions and Canada assigned to and controlled by
GIL MUSIC CORP., 1650 Broadway, New York, NY 10019
International Copyright Secured   All Rights Reserved

Chorus 1	N.C. F#7 B7
	I wanna be your man,
	
	           E C#7
	I wanna be your man.
	
	        F#7 B7
	I wanna be your man,
	
	           E E11
	I wanna be your ma - an.

Verse 3	E E11 E E11 Tell me that you love me, baby, E E11 E E11 Let me under-stand. E E11 E E11 Tell me that you love me, baby, E E11 E7 I wanna be your man.
Verse 4	*Repeat Verse 1*
Chorus 2	*Repeat Chorus 1*
Solo	‖: E E11 |E E11 |E E11 |E E11:‖ *Play 3 times*
Verse 5	*Repeat Verse 1*
Verse 6	*Repeat Verse 2*
Chorus 3	*Repeat Chorus 1*
Outro	E E11 E E11 E ‖: I wanna be your man. :‖ *Repeat and fade*

I Want to Hold Your Hand

Words and Music by John Lennon
and Paul McCartney

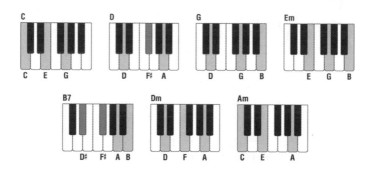

Intro   C D | C D | C D | |

Verse 1

               G   **D**
Oh yeah, I tell you something,

      Em   **B7**
I think you'll under-stand.

           G   **D**
When I say that something,

      Em   **B7**
I wanna hold your hand.

Chorus 1

           C   **D**   **G** **Em**
I wanna hold your hand,

        C   **D**   **G**
I wanna hold your hand.

Copyright © 1963 NORTHERN SONGS LTD.
Copyright Renewed
All Rights in the United States and Canada Controlled and Administered by SONGS OF UNIVERSAL, INC.
All Rights Reserved   Used by Permission

Verse 2

      G   D
Oh please, say to me

Em   B7
  You'll let me be your man.

      G   D
And please say to me

Em   B7
  You'll let me hold your hand.

Chorus 2

C   D   G   Em
  Now let me hold your hand,

C   D   G
  I wanna hold your hand.

Bridge 1

Dm   G
  And when I touch you

     C   Am
I feel happy in-side.

Dm   G
  It's such a feeling

      C   D
That my love I can't hide,

C   D   C   D
I can't hide, I can't hide.

Verse 3	**G**　　　**D** Yeah, you got that something,
	Em　　　　　**B7** I think you'll under-stand.
	G　　**D** When I say that something,
	Em　　　　　**B7** I wanna hold your hand.
Chorus 3	*Repeat Chorus 1*
Bridge 2	*Repeat Bridge 1*
Verse 4	**G**　　　**D** Yeah, you got that something,
	Em　　　　　**B7** I think you'll under-stand.
	G　　**D** When I feel that something,
	Em　　　　　**B7** I wanna hold your hand.
Chorus 4	**C**　　**D**　　**G**　**Em** I wanna hold your hand.
	C　　**D**　　**B7** I wanna hold your hand.
	C　　**D**　　**C**　**G** I wanna hold your hand.

I'll Get You

Words and Music by John Lennon
and Paul McCartney

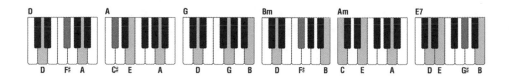

Intro

    D   **A**
Oh yeah, oh yeah,

    D   **A**
Oh yeah, oh yeah.

Verse 1

    D
I-magine I'm in love with you,

    G   **A**
It's easy 'cause I know.

    D   **Bm**
I've i-magined I'm in love with you

G   **A**
Many, many, many times be-fore.

    D   **Am**
It's not like me to pre-tend,

    D   **Bm**
But I'll get you, I'll get you in the end.

    G   **A**
Yes, I will, I'll get you in the end,

    D   **A**
Oh yeah, oh yeah.

Copyright © 1963, 1964 Sony/ATV Music Publishing LLC
Copyright Renewed
All Rights Administered by Sony/ATV Music Publishing LLC, 8 Music Square West, Nashville, TN 37203
International Copyright Secured   All Rights Reserved

Verse 2

D
I think about you night and day,

G   A
I need you and it's true.

D   Bm
When I think about you, I can say,

G   A
I'm never, never, never, never blue.

D   Am
So I'm telling you, my friend,

D   Bm
That I'll get you, I'll get you in the end,

G   A
Yes, I will, I'll get you in the end,

D   A
Oh yeah, oh yeah.

Bridge

G
Well, there's gonna be a time,

D
When I'm gonna change your mind.

E7   A
So you might as well resign yourself to me,

Oh yeah.

Verse 3

       D
I-magine I'm in love with you,

    G   **A**
It's easy 'cause I know.

       D   **Bm**
I've i-magined I'm in love with you

G   **A**
Many, many, many times be-fore.

       D   **Am**
It's not like me to pre-tend,

       D   **Bm**
But I'll get you, I'll get you in the end.

     G   **A**
Yes, I will, I'll get you in the end,

     D   **A**
Oh yeah, oh yeah,

     D   **A**   **D**
Oh yeah, oh yeah, oh yeah.

I Want to Tell You

Words and Music by
George Harrison

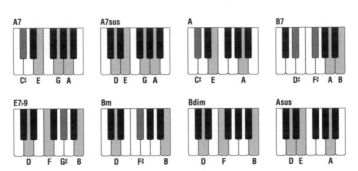

Intro | A7 | A7sus | A7 | A7sus |

Verse 1

    A

   I want to tell you,

         B7

My head is filled with things to say.

E7♭9

   When you're here,

            A7

All those words, they seem to slip away.

    A

Verse 2   When I get near you,

         B7

The games begin to drag me down.

E7♭9

   It's alright,

         A7

I'll make you maybe next time around.

Copyright © 1966 Sony/ATV Music Publishing LLC
Copyright Renewed
All Rights Administered by Sony/ATV Music Publishing LLC, 8 Music Square West, Nashville, TN 37203
International Copyright Secured   All Rights Reserved

Bridge 1	**Bm** **Bdim** **A** But if I seem to act un-kind,

        B7   **Bm**
It's only me, it's not my mind,

Bdim   **A**   **Asus**
That is con-fusing things.

Verse 3	**A** I want to tell you,

               B7
I feel hung up and I don't know why.

E7♭9
  I don't mind, I could wait forever,

A7
I've got time.

Bridge 2	**Bm** **Bdim** **A** Sometimes I wish I knew you well,

           B7   **Bm**
Then I could speak my mind and tell you,

Bdim   **A**   **Asus**
Maybe you'd under-stand.

Verse 4	**A** I want to tell you,

               B7
I feel hung up and I don't know why.

E7♭9
  I don't mind, I could wait forever,

A7
I've got time.

I've got time.

I've got time.   ***Fade out***

I Want You
(She's So Heavy)

Words and Music by John Lennon
and Paul McCartney

Melody:

I want you.   I want you so...

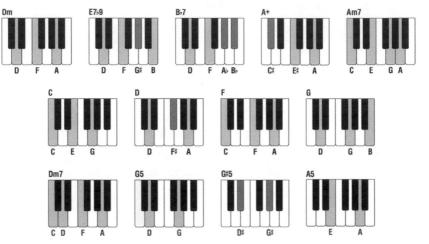

Intro |Dm |Dm/F |E7♭9 |B♭7 |A+ |N.C. |

Verse 1

          Am7
I want you. I want you so bad.

                      C
I want you. I want you so bad,

    D   F
It's driving me mad,

    G   Am7
It's driving me mad.

    Dm7
I want you. I want you so bad, babe.

                      F
I want you. I want you so bad,

    C   B♭7
It's driving me mad,

    G5 G#5 A5
It's driv - ing me mad.

Copyright © 1969 Sony/ATV Music Publishing LLC
Copyright Renewed
All Rights Administered by Sony/ATV Music Publishing LLC, 8 Music Square West, Nashville, TN 37203
International Copyright Secured   All Rights Reserved

| *Interlude 1* | $\mid$ E7♭9 $\mid$ N.C. $\mid$ E7♭9 $\mid$ N.C. $\mid$ E7♭9 $\mid$ N.C. $\mid$ |

Verse 2

      Am7
I want you. I want you so bad, babe.

                            C
I want you. I want you so bad,

   D   **F**
It's driving me mad,

   G   **Am7**
It's driving me mad.

   Dm7
I want you. I want you so bad.

                             F
I want you. I want you so bad,

   C   **B♭7**
It's driving me mad,

   G5   **G♯5 A5**
It's driv - ing me...

| *Interlude 2* | $\mid$ E7♭9 $\mid$ N.C. $\mid$ E7♭9 $\mid$ N.C. $\mid$ E7♭9 $\mid$ N.C. $\mid$ |

Chorus 1

N.C.   Dm Dm/F E7♭9
She's so…

B♭7 A+
Heavy.

Dm   Dm/F E7♭9 B♭7 A+
Heavy. (Heavy, heavy.)

Solo

Am7					
C	D F	G	Am7		
Dm7					
F	C B♭	G5 G♯5 A5			
E7♭9	N.C.	E7♭9	N.C.	E7♭9	N.C.

Chorus 2

N.C.   Dm Dm/F E7♭9
She's so…

B♭7 A+
Heavy.

Dm   Dm/F E7♭9 B♭7 A+
She's so heavy. (Heavy, heavy.)

Verse 3

       Am7
I want you. I want you so bad.

                    C
I want you. I want you so bad,

   D   **F**
It's driving me mad,

   G   **Am7**
It's driving me mad.

   Dm7
I want you.

You know I want you so bad, babe.

I want you.

                   F
You know I want you so bad,

   C   **B♭7**
It's driving me mad,

   G5 **G♯5 A5**
It's driv - ing me mad.

Interlude 3

| E7♭9 | | N.C. | E7♭9 | | N.C. | E7♭9 | | N.C. |

She's so...

Outro

‖: Dm | Dm/F | E7♭9 | B♭7 | A+ :‖ *Play 14 times*

I Will

Words and Music by John Lennon
and Paul McCartney

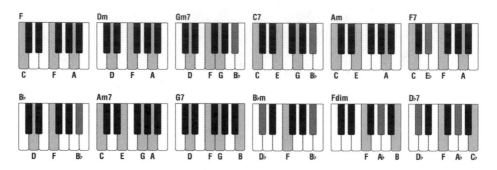

Verse 1

| | F | Dm | Gm7 | C7 |
Who knows how long I've loved you?

| | F | Dm | Am |
You know I love you still.

F7 | Bb | C7 | Dm | F
Will I wait a lonely lifetime?

| | Bb | C7 | F | Dm | Gm7 | C7 |
If you want me to, I will.

Verse 2

| | F | Dm | Gm7 | C7 |
For if I ever saw you,

| | F | Dm | Am |
I didn't catch your name.

F7 | Bb | C7 | Dm | F
But it never really mattered;

| | Bb | C7 | F | F7 |
I will always feel the same.

Copyright © 1968 Sony/ATV Music Publishing LLC
Copyright Renewed
All Rights Administered by Sony/ATV Music Publishing LLC, 8 Music Square West, Nashville, TN 37203
International Copyright Secured   All Rights Reserved

Bridge	**B♭** **Am7 Dm** Love you forever and forever, **Gm7** **C7** **F F7** Love you with all my heart. **B♭** **Am7** **Dm** Love you whenever we're together, **G7** **C7** Love you when we're apart.

Verse 3	**F** **Dm Gm7 C7**
	And when at last I find you,
	
	     F **Dm** **Am**
	Your song will fill the air.
	
	F7 **B♭** **C7** **Dm** **B♭m F**
	Sing it loud so I can hear you.
	
	     B♭ C7 **Dm** **B♭m F**
	Make it easy to be near you.
	
	     B♭ **C7**
	For the things you do
	
	 Dm B♭m F **Fdim**
	Endear you to me,
	
	Gm7 **C7** **D♭7**
	Ah, you know I will,
	
	    F **F7**
	I will.

Outro	|**B♭** **Am** |**Dm** |**Gm7 C7** |**F**

I'll Be Back

Words and Music by John Lennon
and Paul McCartney

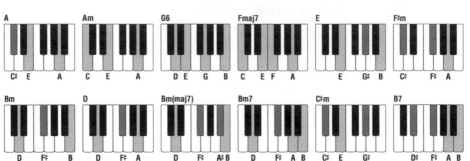

Intro | A | | |

Verse 1

    Am   G6   Fmaj7
You know, if you break my heart I'll go,

    E   A
But I'll be back a-gain.

    Am   G6   Fmaj7
'Cause I told you once before good-bye,

    E   A
But I came back a-gain.

Bridge 1

           F#m
I love you so,

           Bm
I'm the one who wants you.

              E
Yes, I'm the one who wants you.

D   E   D   E
Oh, ho, oh, ho.

Copyright © 1964 Sony/ATV Music Publishing LLC
Copyright Renewed
All Rights Administered by Sony/ATV Music Publishing LLC, 8 Music Square West, Nashville, TN 37203
International Copyright Secured   All Rights Reserved

Verse 2

     Am   **G6**   **Fmaj7**
You could find better things to do

         E   **A**
Than to break my heart a-gain.

         Am   **G6**   **Fmaj7**
This time I will try to show you that I'm

      E   **A**
Not trying to pre-tend.

Bridge 2

Bm **Bm(maj7)** **Bm7**
I

                 C♯m
Thought that you would realize,

   F♯m
That if I ran away from you,

   B7
That you would want me too,

   D   **E**
But I got a big sur-prise,

D   **E**   **D**   **E**
Oh, ho, oh, ho.

Verse 3   *Repeat Verse 2*

Bridge 3

      F♯m
I wanna go,

         Bm
But I hate to leave you.

              E
You know I hate to leave you.

D   **E**   **D**   **E**
Oh, ho, oh, ho.

Outro

Am   **G6**   **Fmaj7**
You, if you break my heart I'll go,

    E   **A**
But I'll be back a-gain.

‖: **A** | | **Am** | :‖ *Repeat and fade*

I'll Cry Instead

Words and Music by John Lennon
and Paul McCartney

Melody: I've got ___ ev-'ry rea-son on earth... ___

Intro |G   C6 |

Verse 1

   G C6 G C6
    I've got every reason
    G C6 G C6 G C6
  On earth to be mad
      G   C6 G C6 D7
    'Cause I've just lost the only girl I had.
      C7
    And if I could get my way,

    I'd get myself locked up today,
      G   C6   D7 G C6 G C6
    But I can't, ___ so I'll cry in-stead.

Verse 2

       G   C6
    I've got a chip on my shoulder
      G   C6 G C6 G C6
    That's bigger than my feet.
    G   C6 G   C6 D7
    I can't talk to people that I meet.
      C7
    If I could see you now,

    I'd try to make you sad somehow,
      G   C6   D7 G C6 G C6
    But I can't, ___ so I'll cry in-stead.

Copyright © 1964 Sony/ATV Music Publishing LLC
Copyright Renewed
All Rights Administered by Sony/ATV Music Publishing LLC, 8 Music Square West, Nashville, TN 37203
International Copyright Secured   All Rights Reserved

Bridge 1

                    Bm
Don't want to cry when there's people there,

        A7
I get shy when they start to stare.

        D
I'm gonna lock myself away,

        E7   **A**   **D**
But I'll come back again some day.

Verse 3

                    G
And when I do,

        C6 **G** **C6** **G** **C6** **G** **C6**
You better hide all the girls,

G   **C6**   **G**   **C6**   **D7**
I'm gonna break their hearts all 'round the world.

        C7
Yes, I'm gonna break them in two,

N.C.
Show you what your lovin' man can do,

        G   **D7** **G**   **C6** **G** **C6**
Until then I'll cry in-stead.

Bridge 2   *Repeat Bridge 1*

Verse 4

                    G
And when I do,

        C6 **G** **C6** **G** **C6** **G** **C6**
You better hide all the girls,

G   **C6**   **G**   **C6**   **D7**
I'm gonna break their hearts all 'round the world.

        C7
Yes, I'm gonna break them in two,

N.C.
Show you what your lovin' man can do,

        G   **D7** **G**   **C6** **G** **C6**
Until then I'll cry in-stead.

I'll Follow the Sun

Words and Music by John Lennon
and Paul McCartney

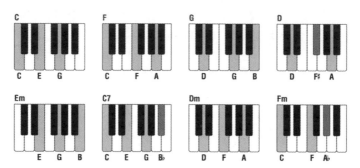

Intro		| C | F C |

Verse 1

> G   F
> One day you'll look
>
> C   D
> To see I've gone,
>
>   C   Em/B   D
> For to-morrow may rain, so
>
>   G   C   F C
> I'll follow the sun.

Verse 2

> G   F
> Some day you'll know
>
> C   D
> I was the one,
>
>   C   Em/B   D
> But to-morrow may rain, so
>
>   G   C   C7
> I'll follow the sun.

Copyright © 1964 Sony/ATV Music Publishing LLC
Copyright Renewed
All Rights Administered by Sony/ATV Music Publishing LLC, 8 Music Square West, Nashville, TN 37203
International Copyright Secured   All Rights Reserved

Bridge 1

          Dm
And now the time has come,

       Fm   **C**   **C7**
And so, my love, I must go.

          Dm
And though I lose a friend

Fm   **C**   **Dm**
In the end you will know, oh.

Verse 3

G   **F**
One day you'll find

C   **D**
  That I have gone,

       C   **Em/B** **D**
But to-morrow may rain, so

  G   **C** **F** **C**
I'll follow the sun.

Solo

|**G** |**F** |**C** |**D** |

       C   **Em/B** **D**
Yes, to-morrow may rain, so

  G   **C** **C7**
I'll follow the sun.

Bridge 2

Repeat Bridge 1

Verse 4

G   **F**
One day you'll find

C   **D**
  That I have gone,

       C   **Em/B** **D**
But to-morrow may rain, so

  G   **C** **F** **C**
I'll follow the sun.

I'm a Loser

Words and Music by John Lennon
and Paul McCartney

Melody:

I'm a los - er.

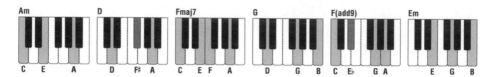

Am   D   Fmaj7   G   F(add9)   Em

C E A   D F# A   C E F A   D G B   C Eb G A   E G B

Intro

   Am D
I'm a los - er.

   Am D
I'm a los - er,

    Am   **Fmaj7 D**
And I'm not what I ap-pear to be.

Verse 1

  G **D** **F(add9)** **G**
 Of all the love I have won or have lost,

     D   **F(add9)** **G**
There is one love I should never have crossed.

    D **F(add9)** **G**
She was a girl in a million, my friend,

     D   **F(add9) G**
I should have known she would win in the end.

Chorus 1

   Am D
I'm a los - er,

   Am   **D**
And I lost someone who's near to me.

  G **Em**
I'm a los - er,

   Am   **Fmaj7 D**
And I'm not what I ap-pear to be.

Copyright © 1964 Sony/ATV Music Publishing LLC
Copyright Renewed
All Rights Administered by Sony/ATV Music Publishing LLC, 8 Music Square West, Nashville, TN 37203
International Copyright Secured   All Rights Reserved

Verse 2

G   D   F(add9) G
Although I laugh and I act like a clown,

                    D   F(add9) G
Beneath this mask I am wearing a frown.

                    D   F(add9)   G
My tears are falling like rain from the sky,

                D   F(add9)   G
Is it for her or myself that I cry?

Chorus 2   *Repeat Chorus 1*

Solo 1

```
‖: G      | D        | F(add9) | G        :‖
   | Am     | D        | Am      | D         |
   | G      | Em       | Am      | Fmaj7 D |
```

Verse 3

G   D   F(add9)   G
What have I done to deserve such a fate?

          D   F(add9) G
I real-ize I have left it too late.

                  D   F(add9) G
And so it's true, pride comes before a fall,

                  D   F(add9)   G
I'm telling you so that you won't lose all.

Chorus 3   *Repeat Chorus 1*

Solo 2

```
‖: G      | D        | F(add9) | G        :‖
   | Am     | D        | Am      | D         |
   | G      | Em       Fade out
```

I'm Down

Words and Music by John Lennon
and Paul McCartney

Verse 1

N.C.
You tell lies thinkin' I can't see,

G   N.C.
You can't cry 'cause you're laughing at me.

Chorus 1

C7
I'm down, (I'm really down.)

G
I'm down. (Down on the ground.)

C7
I'm down. (I'm really down.)

D7   G   N.C.
How can you laugh when you know I'm down?

D7   G   N.C.
(How can you laugh?) When you know I'm down?

Verse 2

G   N.C.
Man buys ring, woman throws it away.

G   N.C.
Same old thing happen every day.

Chorus 2

Repeat Chorus 1

Copyright © 1965 Sony/ATV Music Publishing LLC
Copyright Renewed
All Rights Administered by Sony/ATV Music Publishing LLC, 8 Music Square West, Nashville, TN 37203
International Copyright Secured   All Rights Reserved

Solo 1	|G			|C7		
	|G	|D7	|G		

Verse 3

G   N.C.
We're all alone and there's nobody else.

G   N.C.
You still moan, keep your hands to yourself.

Chorus 3   *Repeat Chorus 1*

Solo 2	|G			|C7		
		G		D7	C7	G	D7	

Outro

                                                           G
‖: Oh babe, you know I'm down, (I'm really down,)

Oh yes, I'm down, (I'm really down,)

             C7
I'm down on the ground, (I'm really down,)

   G
I'm down, (I'm really down.)

              D7   C7
Ah, baby, I'm upside   down.

          G   D7
Oh yeah, yeah, yeah, yeah, yeah. :‖   ***Repeat and fade***

I'm Looking Through You

Words and Music by John Lennon
and Paul McCartney

Melody:

I'm look-ing through   you, __

Intro | G | Gmaj9 | G   C | G   C | G   C |

Verse 1

G   C   G/B Am   Em   D
I'm look-ing through you,   where did you go?

G C   G/B Am   Em   D
I thought I   knew you,   what did I know?

Em7   Asus Am   G   C   D
You don't look differ - ent, but you have changed.

G   C   G/B Am   C   G   C
I'm look-ing   through you,   you're not the same.

| G   C | G   C |

Verse 2

G   C G/B Am   Em   D
Your lips are moving,   I cannot hear;

G   C   G/B Am   Em   D
Your voice is   soothing,   but the words aren't clear.

Em7   Asus Am   G   C D
You don't sound differ - ent, I've learnt the game.

G   C   G/B Am   C   G   C
I'm look-ing   through you,   you're not the same.

| G   C | G   C | G |

Copyright © 1965 Sony/ATV Music Publishing LLC
Copyright Renewed
All Rights Administered by Sony/ATV Music Publishing LLC, 8 Music Square West, Nashville, TN 37203
International Copyright Secured   All Rights Reserved

Bridge 1

```
C                          G
Why, tell my why did you not treat me right?

C                      Dsus        D
Love has a nasty habit of disappearing overnight.
```

Verse 3

```
G      C    G/B Am Em            D
You're think-ing   of me   the same old way;

G     C    G/B  Am      Em          D
You were a  -   bove me,   but not to-day.

Em7      Asus  Am    G     C    D
The only differ - ence is you're down there.

G     C   G/B Am          C              G    C
I'm look-ing   through you   and you're no-where.
```
```
|G    C  |G    C  |G        |
```

Bridge 2   *Repeat Bridge 1*

Verse 4

```
G    C   G/B Am      Em            D
I'm look-ing  through you,   where did you go?

G  C     G/B Am      Em          D
I thought I    knew you,    what did I know?

Em7            Asus  Am    G   C   D
You don't look differ - ent, but you have changed.

G    C   G/B Am          C              G    C
I'm look-ing  through you,   you're not the same.
```

Outro

```
G        C         G      C
Yeah! Well, baby, you've changed.

G  C         G    C
Ah,  I'm looking through you.

G  C         G     C G  C
Yeah,  I'm looking through you.        *Fade out*
```

I'm Only Sleeping

Words and Music by John Lennon
and Paul McCartney

Melody:

When I wake up ear - ly in the morn - ing, _

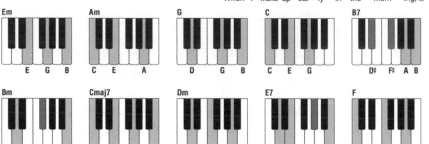

Verse 1

Em   Am
When I wake up early in the morning,

G C G   B7
Lift my head, I'm still yawning.

Em   Am
When I'm in the middle of a dream,

G C G   C
Stay in bed, float up-stream.

(Float upstream.)

Chorus 1

G   Am
Please don't wake me, no, don't shake me.

Bm   Am   Cmaj7
Leave me where I am, I'm only sleeping.

Verse 2

Em   Am
Everybody seems to think I'm lazy.

G C G   B7
I don't mind, I think they're crazy.

Em   Am
Running everywhere at such a speed,

G C G   C
Till they find there's no need.

(There's no need.)

Copyright © 1966 Sony/ATV Music Publishing LLC
Copyright Renewed
All Rights Administered by Sony/ATV Music Publishing LLC, 8 Music Square West, Nashville, TN 37203
International Copyright Secured   All Rights Reserved

Chorus 2

G   Am   Bm
Please don't spoil my day, I'm miles a-way,

            Am   Cmaj7 Em
And after all, I'm only sleeping.

Bridge 1

Dm   E7   Am   Am/G
Keeping an eye on the world going by my window.

F
Taking my time.

E7   Am
Lying there and staring at the ceiling,

G   C   G   B7
Waiting for a sleepy feeling.

Solo

| Em | Am | G C | G C | | |

Chorus 3

G   Am   Bm
Please don't spoil my day, I'm miles a-way,

            Am   Cmaj7 Em
And after all, I'm only sleeping.

Bridge 2

Dm   E7   Am   Am/G
Keeping an eye on the world going by my window,

F
Taking my time.

Verse 3

Repeat Verse 1

Chorus 4

G   Am
Please don't wake me, no, don't shake me.

Bm   Am   Cmaj7   Em
Leave me where I am, I'm only sleeping.

I'm So Tired

Words and Music by John Lennon
and Paul McCartney

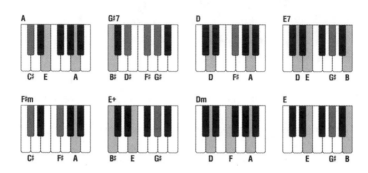

Verse 1

    A G♯7   D   E7
I'm so tired, I haven't slept a wink.

    A F♯m D   E7
I'm so tired,   my mind is on the blink.

    A   E+
I wonder should I get up

    F♯m   Dm
And fix myself a drink?

No, no, no.

Verse 2

    A G♯7   D   E7
I'm so tired, I don't know what to do.

    A F♯m D   E7
I'm so tired,   my mind is set on you.

    A   E+
I wonder should I call you,

    F♯m   Dm
But I know what you would do.

Copyright © 1968, 1969 Sony/ATV Music Publishing LLC
Copyright Renewed
All Rights Administered by Sony/ATV Music Publishing LLC, 8 Music Square West, Nashville, TN 37203
International Copyright Secured All Rights Reserved

Chorus 1

A
You'd say I'm putting you on,

But it's no joke, it's doing me harm.

    E
You know I can't sleep, I can't stop my brain.

You know it's three weeks, I'm going insane.

    D
You know I'd give you everything I've got

     A
For a little peace of mind.

Verse 3

   A G#7 D   E7
I'm so tired, I'm feeling so up-set.

  A F#m   D   E7
Al-though I'm so tired, I'll have another cigarette.

  A   E+
And curse Sir Walter Raleigh,

   F#m   Dm
He was such a stupid get.

Chorus 2   *Repeat Chorus 1*

Outro

   D
I'd give you everything I've got

    A
For a little peace of mind.

   D
I'd give you everything I've got

    A
For a little peace of mind.

I've Got a Feeling

Words and Music by John Lennon
and Paul McCartney

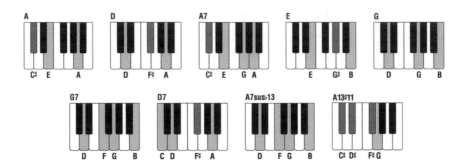

Intro

| A   D/A | A   D/A |

Verse 1

    A   D/A A   D/A
I've got a feel-ing, a feeling deep in-side.

        A D/A A   D/A
Oh yeah,   oh yeah, that's right.

A   D/A A   D/A
  I've got a feel-ing, a feeling I can't hide.

     A   D/A   A D/A A
Oh no, no,   oh no,   oh no.

A7   E   G D
Yeah, yeah,

N.C.   A   D/A A D/A
I've got a feel-ing, yeah!

Copyright © 1970 Sony/ATV Music Publishing LLC
Copyright Renewed
All Rights Administered by Sony/ATV Music Publishing LLC, 8 Music Square West, Nashville, TN 37203
International Copyright Secured   All Rights Reserved

PIANO CHORD SONGBOOK

Verse 2

   A   D/A   A   D/A
   Oh, please be-lieve me, I'd hate to miss the train.

    A D/A A   D/A
Oh yeah,   oh yeah.

   A   D/A   A   D/A
   And if you leave me, I won't be late again.

    A D/A A D/A
Oh no, oh no, oh no.

   A7   E G D N.C.   D/A
   Yeah, yeah!   I've got a feeling, yeah!

   A   D/A
   I've got a feel-ing.

Bridge

 E
All these years I've been wandering around,

 G7
Wondering how come nobody told me

 D7
All that I've been looking for was

                       A7   N.C.
Somebody who looked like you.

Verse 3

   A   D/A   A   D/A
   I've got a feel-ing that keeps me on my toes.

    A D/A A   D/A
Oh yeah,   oh yeah.

   A   D/A   A   D/A
   I've got a feeling, I think that everybody knows.

     A D/A   A D/A A7
Oh yeah,   oh yeah,   oh yeah.

        E G D N.C.   A   D/A A D/A
   Yeah, yeah!   I've got a feel-ing, yeah!

Verse 4

   A   D/A
   Everybody had a hard year,

   A   D/A
Everybody had a good time.

   A   D/A
Everybody had a wet dream,

   A   D/A
Everybody saw the sunshine.

    A
Oh yeah, (Oh yeah.)

    D/A   A D/A
Oh yeah, oh yeah.

Verse 5	A D/A
	Everybody had a good year,

A   D/A
Everybody let their hair down.

A   D/A
Everybody pulled their socks up,

A   D/A
Everybody put their foot down.

Interlude |A7 A7sus♭13   A13♯11 |A7   A13♯11 A7sus♭13 |
Yeah.
|A   D/A |A   D/A |

A   D/A
Verse 6   Everybody had a good year,

A   D/A
Everybody had a hard time.

A   D/A
Everybody had a wet dream,

A   D/A
Everybody saw the sunshine.

A   D/A
Verse 7   Everybody had a good year,

A   D/A
Everybody let their hair down.

A   D/A
Everybody pulled their socks up,

A   D/A
Everybody put their foot down.

Oh yeah.

Outro | A7 A7sus♭13   A13♯11 | A7   A13♯11 A7sus♭13 |
(Yeah.)   (I've got a feeling.)
‖: A7 A7sus♭13   A13♯11 | A7   A13♯11 A7sus♭13 :‖
(I've got a feeling.)

It's All Too Much

Words and Music by
George Harrison

Melody:

It's   all   too   much. _____

C   C   E   G

G   D   G   B

G(add9)   D   G A B

Intro   ‖: C   G | G(add9) G | C   G G(add9) | G :‖ *Play 3 times*

‖: C/G G | G(add9) G | C/G G G(add9) | G :‖

It's all too much.

Verse 1
G
   When I look into your eyes,

Your love is there for me.

And the more I go inside,

The more there is to see.

Chorus 1
   C/G   G   G(add9) G
It's all too much for me to   take,

    C/G   G   G(add9) G
The love that's shining all   a - round you.

C/G G   G(add9)   G
Every-where, it's what you make,

   C/G G
For us to take,

   G(add9) G
It's all too   much.

Copyright © 1968, 1969 Sony/ATV Music Publishing LLC
Copyright Renewed
All Rights Administered by Sony/ATV Music Publishing LLC, 8 Music Square West, Nashville, TN 37203
International Copyright Secured   All Rights Reserved

Verse 2

G
Floating down the stream of time

From life to life with me.

Makes no difference where you are,

Or where you'd like to be.

Chorus 2

  C/G G   G(add9) G
It's all too much for me to take,

  C/G   G   G(add9) G
The love that's shining all   a - round here.

C/G G   G(add9) G
All the world is birthday cake,

  C/G G
So take a piece

  G(add9) G
But not too much.

Solo

‖: C/G G |G(add9) G |

| C/G G G(add9) |G   :‖

Verse 3

G
Sail me on a silver sun

Where I know that I'm free.

Show me that I'm everywhere,

And get me home for tea.

Chorus 3

       C/G G   G(add9) G
It's all too much for me to   see,

        C/G   G   G(add9) G
The love that's shining all a - round here.

        C/G G   G(add9) G
The more I learn, the less I   know,

        C/G G
And what I do,

     G(add9) G
Is all too   much.

Chorus 4   *Repeat Chorus 1*

Outro

| C/G G | G(add9) G | C/G G G(add9) | G | |
It's too much.   Ah.

| C/G G | G(add9) G | C/G G G(add9) | G | |
It's too much.

‖: C/G G | G(add9) G | C/G G G(add9) | G :‖

        C/G   G
With your long blonde hair

        G(add9) G
And your eyes of blue...

| C/G G G(add9) | G | |

        C/G   G
With your long blonde hair

        G(add9) G
And your eyes of blue...

| C/G G G(add9) | G | |

| C/G G | G(add9) G | C/G G G(add9) | G | |
You're too much, ah.

‖: C/G G | G(add9) G | C/G G G(add9) | G :‖

‖: C/G G   G(add9) G :‖ *Repeat and fade*
Too much, too   much.

I've Just Seen a Face

Words and Music by John Lennon
and Paul McCartney

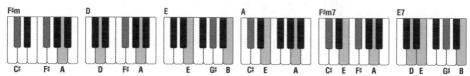

Intro | F#m | | | D |
| | | | E | |

Verse 1

  A
I've just seen a face,

                                  F#m
I can't forget the time or place where we just met.

She's just the girl for me

                      F#m7   D
And I want all the world to see we've met.

          E   A
Mm, mm, mm, mm, mm, mm.

Verse 2

  A
Had it been another day

I might have looked the other way

  F#m
And I'd have never been aware,

                F#m7 D
But as it is I'll dream of her to-night,

         E   A
Da, da, da, da, da, da.

Copyright © 1965 Sony/ATV Music Publishing LLC
Copyright Renewed
All Rights Administered by Sony/ATV Music Publishing LLC, 8 Music Square West, Nashville, TN 37203
International Copyright Secured   All Rights Reserved

Chorus 1

E   D
Falling, yes I am falling,
      A D   A
And she keeps calling me back again.

Verse 3

A
I have never known the like of this,

I've been alone and I have
F#m
Missed things and kept out of sight,
         F#m7 D
But other girls were never quite like this,
     E   A
Da, da, da, da, da, da.

Chorus 2   *Repeat Chorus 1*

Solo

| A | | | | F#m | | |
| | | F#m7 | D | | E | A | |

Chorus 3   *Repeat Chorus 1*

Verse 4

A
I've just seen a face,
              F#m
I can't forget the time or place where we just met.

She's just the girl for me
        F#m7 D
And I want all the world to see we've met.
     E   A
Mm, mm, mm, da, da, da.

Chorus 4   *Repeat Chorus 1*

Chorus 5   *Repeat Chorus 1*

Outro

E   D
Oh, falling, yes I am falling,
      A D   E A
And she keeps calling me back again.

If I Fell

Words and Music by John Lennon
and Paul McCartney

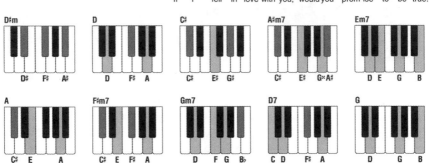

Intro

      D♯m
If I fell in love with you,

      D
Would you promise to be true

    C♯   **A♯m7**
And help me understand?

      D♯m
'Cause I've been in love before,

     D
And I found that love was more

    Em7   **A**
Than just holding hands.

Verse 1

    D **Em7 F♯m7** **Em7**
If I give my   heart to you,

    A
I must be sure

      D **Em7 F♯m7**   **Em7**
From the ver-y   start, that you

      A   **D** **Gm7** **A**
Would love me more than her.

Copyright © 1964 Sony/ATV Music Publishing LLC
Copyright Renewed
All Rights Administered by Sony/ATV Music Publishing LLC, 8 Music Square West, Nashville, TN 37203
International Copyright Secured   All Rights Reserved

Verse 2

     D   Em7 F#m7 Em7
If I trust in   you, oh please,

     A
Don't run and hide.

     D   Em7 F#m7 Em7
If I love you   too, oh please,

     A   D7
Don't hurt my pride like her.

Bridge 1

D7   G
'Cause I couldn't stand the pain.

     Gm7   D
And I would be sad if our new love

     A
Was in vain.

Verse 3

     D   Em7 F#m7 Em7
So I hope you see that I

     A
Would love to love you.

D Em7 F#m7 Em7
And that   she will cry

     A   D7
When she learns we are two.

Bridge 2   *Repeat Bridge 1*

Verse 4

     D   Em7 F#m7 Em7
So I hope you see that I

     A
Would love to love you.

D Em7 F#m7 Em7
And that   she will cry

     A   D
When she learns we are two.

     Gm7   D Gm7 D
If I fell in love with you.

If I Needed Someone

Words and Music by
George Harrison

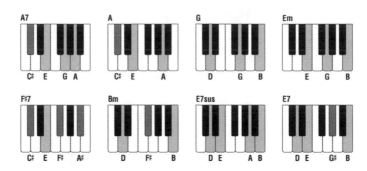

Intro | A7 | | | |

Verse 1

A
If I needed someone to love,

G/A
You're the one that I'd be thinking of,

A7
If I needed someone.

Verse 2

A
If I had more time to spend,

G/A
Then I guess I'd be with you, my friend,

A7
If I needed someone.

Copyright © 1965 Sony/ATV Music Publishing LLC
Copyright Renewed
All Rights Administered by Sony/ATV Music Publishing LLC, 8 Music Square West, Nashville, TN 37203
International Copyright Secured   All Rights Reserved

Bridge 1

Em   F$\sharp$7
Had you come some other day,

                      Bm
Then it might not have been like this,

Em   F$\sharp$7   Bm   E7sus E7
But you see now I'm too much in love.

Verse 3

A
Carve your number on my wall,

                             G/A
And maybe you will get a call from me,

        A7
If I needed someone.

Solo

| A | | | | |
| G/A | | A7 | | |

Verse 4   *Repeat Verse 2*

Bridge 2   *Repeat Bridge 1*

Verse 5   *Repeat Verse 3*

Outro

A7   A
Ah, ah.

If You've Got Trouble

Words and Music by John Lennon
and Paul McCartney

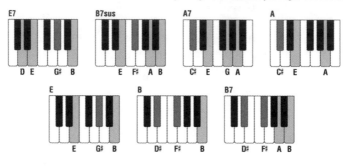

Intro |E7 | | |

Verse 1

E7   B7sus   E7
If you've got trouble, then you've got less trouble than me.

                        B7sus   E7
You say you're worried, you can't be as worried as me.

A7   B7sus
You're quite content to be bad,

A7   B7sus
With all the advantage you had over me.

E7   B7sus   E7
Just 'cause you're troubled, then don't bring your troubles to me.

Verse 2

        E7   B7sus   E7
I don't think it's funny when you ask for money and things.

                        B7sus   E7
Especially when you're standing there wearing diamonds and rings.

A7   B7sus
You think I'm soft in the head,

        A7   B7sus
Well, try someone softer in-stead, pretty thing.

E7   B7sus   E7
It's not so funny when you know what money can bring.

Copyright © 1965 Sony/ATV Music Publishing LLC
Copyright Renewed
All Rights Administered by Sony/ATV Music Publishing LLC, 8 Music Square West, Nashville, TN 37203
International Copyright Secured   All Rights Reserved

Bridge 1

A   E
 You better leave me a-lone,

A E B E
I don't need a thing from you.

A   E
 You better take yourself home,

A E B E
Go and count a ring or two.

Verse 3

E7   B7sus   E7
If you've got trouble then you've got less trouble than me.

              B7sus   E7
You say you're worried, you can't be as worried as me.

A7   B7sus
You're quite content to be bad,

A7   B7sus
With all the advantage you had over me.

E7   B7sus   E7
Just 'cause you're troubled, then don't bring your troubles to me.

(Oh, rock on, anybody!)

Solo |E | | |A7 | |

      |E | |B7 |A7 |E | |

Bridge 2 *Repeat Bridge 1*

Verse 4

E7   B7sus   E7
If you've got trouble then you've got less trouble than me.

              B7sus   E7
You say you're worried, you can't be as worried as me.

A7   B7sus
You're quite content to be bad,

A7   B7sus
With all the advantage you had over me.

E7   B7sus   E7
Just 'cause you're troubled, then don't bring your troubles to me.

E7   B7sus   E7 E
Just 'cause you're troubled, then don't bring your troubles to me.

In My Life

Words and Music by John Lennon
and Paul McCartney

Melody:

There are   plac - es   I   re - mem-ber...

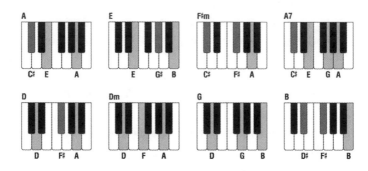

Intro |A |E |A |E |

Verse 1
       A   E   F#m   A7/G
There are places I re-member

       D   Dm   A
All my life, _____ though some have changed.

         E   F#m   A7/G
Some forever, not for better,

        D   Dm   A
Some have gone, _____ and some remain.

Chorus 1
        F#m   D
All these places had their moments,

       G   A
With lovers and friends I still can recall,

       F#m   B
Some are dead and some are living,

       Dm   A   E
In my life, I've loved them all.

Copyright © 1965 Sony/ATV Music Publishing LLC
Copyright Renewed
All Rights Administered by Sony/ATV Music Publishing LLC, 8 Music Square West, Nashville, TN 37203
International Copyright Secured   All Rights Reserved

Verse 2

        A   E   F#m A7/G
But of all these friends and lovers,

        D Dm   A
There is no one com-pares with you.

               E   F#m   A7/G
And these memories lose their meaning

        D   Dm   A
When I think of love as something new.

Chorus 2

        F#m   D
Though I know I'll never lose af-fection

     G   A
For people and things that went before,

 F#m   B
I know I'll often stop and think a-bout them.

    Dm   A
In my life, I love you more.

Solo

‖: A   E |F#m A7/G |D Dm |A   :‖

Chorus 3   *Repeat Chorus 2*

Outro

|A |E |Dm   N.C.   A
                     In my life, I love you more.

|E |A   ‖

In Spite of All the Danger

By Paul McCartney
and George Harrison

Melody:

In spite of all the dan - ger,

E
E G# B

B7
D# F# A B

E7
D E G# B

A
C# E A

Intro

| E |

Verse 1

B7   E
In spite of all the danger,

In spite of all that may be,

E7   A
I'll do anything for you.

                    B7
Anything you want me to,

          E   A   E
If you'll be true to me.

Verse 2

                    E
In spite of all the heartache

That you may cause me,

E7   A
I'll do anything for you.

                    B7
Anything you want me to,

          E   A   E   E7
If you'll be true to me.

© 1995 MPL COMMUNICATIONS LTD.
Administered by MPL COMMUNICATIONS, INC.
All Rights Reserved

Bridge

    A   **E**   **E7**

I'll look after you like I've never done be-fore,

    A   **B7**   **N.C.**

I'll keep all the others from knocking at your door.

Verse 3

N.C.   **E**

 In spite of all the danger,

In spite of all that may be,

E7   **A**

 I'll do anything for you.

                  B7

Anything you want me to,

               E **A** **E**

If you'll be true to me.

Solo

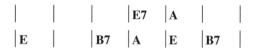

```
|     |     |     | E7 | A  |     |     |
| E   |     | B7  | A  | E  | B7  |
```

Verse 4

               E

In spite of all the heartache

That you may cause me,

E7   **A**

 I'll do anything for you.

                  B7

Anything you want me to,

               E **A** **E** **E7**

If you'll be true to me.

               A

I'll do anything for you.

                  B7

Anything you want me to,

               E **A** **E**

If you'll be true to me.

The Inner Light

Words and Music by
George Harrison

With - out go - ing out of my door, —

Intro ‖: D5 | | | | :‖

Verse 1

   D D7 G/D
With-out going out of my door,

   D D7 Em/D
I can know all things on earth.

   D   D7 Em
With-out looking out of my window,

   D D7 G/D
I can know the ways of heaven.

Chorus 1

   G/D   D
The farther one trav-els,

    D7
The less one knows,

   D   G/D D
The less one really knows.

Copyright © 1968 Sony/ATV Music Publishing LLC
Copyright Renewed
All Rights Administered by Sony/ATV Music Publishing LLC, 8 Music Square West, Nashville, TN 37203
International Copyright Secured   All Rights Reserved

| *Interlude* | ‖: **D5** | | | | | :‖ |

Verse 2

       D   **D7**   **G/D**
With-out going out of your door,

          D   **D7**   **Em/D**
You can know all things on earth.

          D   **D7**   **Em**
With-out looking out of your window,

          D   **D7**   **G/D**
You can know the ways of heaven.

Chorus 2

Repeat Chorus 1

Verse 3

D
Arrive without traveling,

See all without looking,

Do all without doing.

| *Outro* | | **D** | | | **D5** | | | |

It Won't Be Long

Words and Music by John Lennon
and Paul McCartney

Melody:

It won't be long, yeah,

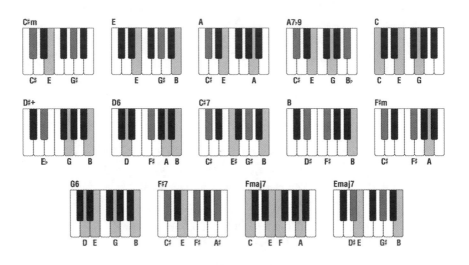

Chorus 1

            C♯m
It won't be long, yeah, yeah, yeah.

            E
It won't be long, yeah, yeah, yeah.

            C♯m
It won't be long, yeah.

    A   **A7♭9** **E**
Till I be-long to you.

Verse 1

         E   **C**   **E**
Every night when everybody has fun,

           C   **E**
Here am I sitting all on my own.

Chorus 2   *Repeat Chorus 1*

Copyright © 1963, 1964 Sony/ATV Music Publishing LLC
Copyright Renewed
All Rights Administered by Sony/ATV Music Publishing LLC, 8 Music Square West, Nashville, TN 37203
International Copyright Secured   All Rights Reserved

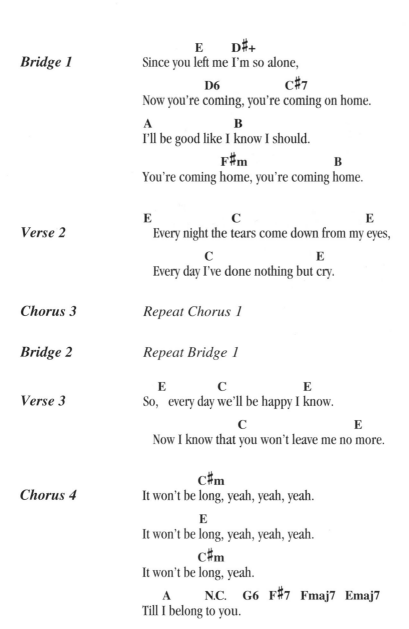

Bridge 1

      E   D#+
Since you left me I'm so alone,

         D6   C#7
Now you're coming, you're coming on home.

  A   B
I'll be good like I know I should.

          F#m   B
You're coming home, you're coming home.

Verse 2

 E   C   E
   Every night the tears come down from my eyes,

       C   E
Every day I've done nothing but cry.

Chorus 3   *Repeat Chorus 1*

Bridge 2   *Repeat Bridge 1*

Verse 3

    E   C   E
So,   every day we'll be happy I know.

           C   E
Now I know that you won't leave me no more.

Chorus 4

      C#m
It won't be long, yeah, yeah, yeah.

      E
It won't be long, yeah, yeah, yeah.

      C#m
It won't be long, yeah.

  A   N.C.   G6 F#7 Fmaj7 Emaj7
Till I belong to you.

It's Only Love

Words and Music by John Lennon
and Paul McCartney

Melody:

I get high when I see you go by.

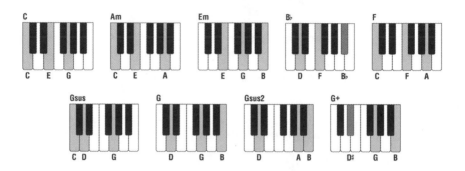

Intro | C | Am | C | Am |

Verse 1

     C Am   Bb F   Gsus G Gsus2 G
I get high when I see you go by.

     G+
My, oh, my.

     C   Em   Bb F   Gsus G Gsus2 G
When you sigh my, my in-side just flies,

     G+
Butterflies.

     F   G   C   Am
Why am I so shy when I'm be-side you?

Copyright © 1965 Sony/ATV Music Publishing LLC
Copyright Renewed
All Rights Administered by Sony/ATV Music Publishing LLC, 8 Music Square West, Nashville, TN 37203
International Copyright Secured   All Rights Reserved

Chorus 1

          B♭   **G**
It's only love and that is all.

                 C   **Am**
Why should I feel the way I do?

          B♭   **G**
It's only love and that is all,

          F   **G**
But it's so hard loving you.

Verse 2

C **Em**   **B♭**   **F**   **Gsus** **G** **Gsus2** **G**
Is it right that you and I should fight

G+
Every night?

C   **Em**   **B♭**   **F**   **Gsus** **G** **Gsus2** **G**
Just the sight of you makes night time bright,

G+
Very bright.

F   **G**   **C**   **Am**
Haven't I the right to make it up, girl?

Chorus 2

          B♭   **G**
It's only love and that is all,

                 C   **Am**
Why should I feel the way I do?

          B♭   **G**
It's only love and that is all,

          F   **G**
But it's so hard loving you.

          F   **G**
Yes, it's so hard loving you,

        C **Am** **C** **Am** **C** **Am** **C**
Loving you.

HAL LEONARD PROUDLY PRESENTS THE
Piano Chord Songbook Series

Play and sing your favorite songs with the Piano Chord Songbook series! These collections include lyrics and piano chord diagrams for dozens of popular hit songs. At 6" x 9", these portable songbooks will come in handy just about anywhere you want to play!

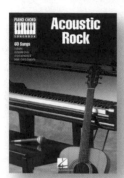   

Acoustic Rock
62 hits, including: Across the Universe • Catch the Wind • Me and Julio Down by the Schoolyard • Night Moves • Seven Bridges Road • Time in a Bottle • and many more.
00311813...$12.95

Children's Songs
80 songs kids love, including: Do-Re-Mi • The Farmer in the Dell • John Jacob Jingleheimer Schmidt • The Muffin Man • Puff the Magic Dragon • and many more.
00311961...$12.99

Country Standards
60 country hits, including: Always on My Mind • Crazy • Deep in the Heart of Texas • El Paso • I Walk the Line • King of the Road • Okie from Muskogee • and more.
00311812...$12.95

Folksongs
80 folk favorites, including: Aura Lee • Camptown Races • Down by the Riverside • Good Night Ladies • Man of Constant Sorrow • Tom Dooley • Water Is Wide • and more.
00311962...$12.99

Jazz Standards
50 songs, including: But Beautiful • Come Rain or Come Shine • Honeysuckle Rose • Misty • The Nearness of You • Stardust • What'll I Do? • and more.
00311963 ....$12.99

Elton John
60 hits from this piano icon, including: Bennie and the Jets • Goodbye Yellow Brick Road • Mona Lisas and Mad Hatters • Tiny Dancer • Your Song • and more.
00311960 ....$12.99

Pop Hits
60 songs, including: All Out of Love • Don't Know Why • Every Breath You Take • More than Words • She's Always a Woman • Time After Time • and more.
00311810...$12.95

Three Chord Songs
58 three-chord classic hits, including: Authority Song • Bad Case of Loving You • Bye Bye Love • Kansas City • La Bamba • Twist and Shout • and more.
00311814...$12.95

1009

FOR MORE INFORMATION, SEE YOUR LOCAL MUSIC DEALER, OR WRITE TO:

Visit Hal Leonard online at
www.halleonard.com

7777 W. BLUEMOUND RD. P.O. BOX 13819 MILWAUKEE, WI 53213